To Nora, a woman of great generosity.

Johnny Doherty, C.ss.R.

LIVING THE SUNDAY LITURGY

Johnny Doherty CSsR

Living the Sunday Liturgy

the columba press

First published in 1995 by
the columba press
93 The Rise, Mount Merrion, Blackrock, Co Dublin, Ireland

Cover by Bill Bolger
Origination by The Columba Press
Printed in Ireland by Colour Books, Ltd, Dublin

ISBN 1 85607 137 5

Contents

Introduction   7

Year A

Section 1   Advent 1 - The Baptism of the Lord   11

Section 2   2nd - 9th Sunday of the Year   23

Section 3   Lent   35

Section 4   Holy Week - Easter Sunday   45

Section 5   Easter 2 - Pentecost   53

Section 6   Trinity Sunday - 15th Sunday of the Year   65

Section 7   16th - 22nd Sunday of the Year   75

Section 8   23rd - 28th Sunday of the Year   85

Section 9   29th Sunday - Christ the King   95

Year B

Section 1   Advent 1 - The Baptism of the Lord   105

Section 2   2nd - 9th Sunday of the Year   117

Section 3   Lent   129

Section 4   Passion Sunday - Easter Sunday   137

Section 5   Easter 2 - Pentecost   145

Section 6   Trinity Sunday - 14th Sunday of the Year   155

Section 7   15th - 22nd Sunday of the Year   165

Section 8   23rd - 28th Sunday of the Year   177

Section 9   29th Sunday - Christ the King   187

Year C

Section 1	Advent 1 - The Baptism of the Lord	197
Section 2	2nd - 8th Sunday of the Year	209
Section 3	Lent	219
Section 4	Passion Sunday - Easter Sunday	229
Section 5	Easter 2 - Pentecost	235
Section 6	Trinity Sunday - 15th Sunday of the Year	247
Section 7	16th - 21st Sunday of the Year	259
Section 8	22nd - 27th Sunday of the Year	269
Section 9	28th Sunday - Christ the King	279

Introduction

Sunday Mass is the centre of the practice of faith for Catholics. It is not the only thing we do, by any means, but it is our main act of worship. Everything else is connected with it in some way. In the past twenty-five years, there have been great efforts to make the Mass more understandable and even enjoyable. But, with all the changes that have taken place, the Sunday Mass continues to be difficult for very many people. The single biggest weakness of our celebration of Mass is that people are not prepared for what is going to take place. This book is presented to help families and individuals to come together on a Sunday really searching for what God wants to give.

Is it always the same?

A mistake a lot of people make is to think that the Mass is always the same. In fact, every Sunday there is a special theme, some particular way of thinking about Christ and ourselves and our world. Very specific graces are prayed for, very definite directions established for the week ahead. We need to be prepared for this.

How long should Mass last?

Answer: For life. The main reason for any individual to go to Mass is to be sent out again to live what has been received. Week by week we are entrusted with the Word of God and empowered to make that word live in our world. We are fed with the Body and Blood of Christ so that we can have the strength and confidence to live for the salvation of our world. The purpose of the Mass is 'that by eating the Body of Christ, we can become the Body of Christ.'

Preparing for each other

Each person is an individual. Christ forms us into one Body. We need to be prepared constantly for this. Unity does not just happen. It has to be made happen by us as we surrender to Christ and learn to love one another.

Sunday Mass is given to us as the major on-going source of renewal of faith, hope and love for the whole church. Even in places where Mass is not possible every Sunday because of the shortage of priests, the liturgy is celebrated often in eucharistic services led by lay women and men. In this part of the world there is still a strong view that the Mass somehow belongs to the priest. It is up to him to put everything into it. If he turns us on by how he does it, or by what he says, we are glad. If he doesn't come up to our expectations, we complain. Of course, the priest has a very special place in the celebration of Mass. A lot does depend on what he puts into it. But the Mass will not really be what it was meant to be until people begin to take responsibility for it. This can best be done by taking time each week to prepare for the Sunday Mass that is coming up.

Some suggestions

There is no one way to prepare for Sunday Mass. If you find a better way than using *Living the Sunday Liturgy*, then please go that way – and let us know about it! The following suggestions are made for getting the most out of this book:

• It can be used by an individual, a couple, a family, a group.

• Establish a regular time each week when you will work on them. Friday or Saturday would seem the best days to aim for.

• Each person should take time first to answer the questions on the page. This is best done by writing down the things that strike you in response to each question.

• Together, as a couple, a family, a group, choose one of the questions that you especially want to get into. Spend most of the time on that. Read the particular passage under which that question is found. Share what you hear from that passage and talk about your answers to the question. Then take some time with the other readings and questions.

• End with the prayer theme for the Sunday. Share a little of your answer to the question under this. Then pray the prayer together.

•Each individual can carry the Sunday Mass right through the following week:

a) By making the response to the psalm – and the psalm itself – part of your prayer through the week.

b) By taking one of the questions each day and developing your response to it more fully. For example:

    1) Sunday: Reflect on the Focus for the Mass.

    2) Monday: Work on the Questions for Action.

    3) Tuesday: The Prayer Theme and question.

    4) Wednesday: The First Reading and question

    5) Thursday: The Second Reading and question.

    6) Friday: The Gospel Reading and question.

    7) Saturday: Prepare for next week.

• In these ways your whole week can be filled with the power of the Sunday Mass. If it is, you will find great growth in your life; great peace in your heart; great joy in your love.

Johnny Doherty CSsR

Year A

Advent 1 - The Baptism of the Lord

Introduction

Welcome to another year of the Church's journey in faith. It can be a very dull journey for those who remain mainly as spectators. It can be a very exciting journey for those who get involved and are part of the creation of a new world.

This first section of the Church's Sunday Liturgy runs from the 1st Sunday in Advent to the Baptism of the Lord. People often think of it as going towards Christmas, and then there is a great anti-climax. When we see it as pointing towards the baptism of the Lord we place the excitement of Christmas in its proper context – the mission of saving the world, of transforming it, is why we have Christmas and that is still going on right into our day and our lives. The child who was born at Christmas still lives with us.

Theme

The main theme of these few weeks is JOY. That's what God wants for us, particularly at this time. That's what is on offer from his grace. There is the joy of waiting through the four weeks of Advent as all the preparations for Christmas take place – the shopping, the cards, the decorating, the partying, the praying. There is the joy of Christmas Midnight Mass and Christmas morning with the song of the angels, the opening of presents, the delight of the children, the hugs and the kisses of appreciation. There's the joy of waiting to hear what this child will be, anointed to give his life for our salvation and the salvation of the world. Families are united, old friends are contacted, new friends are made, a new year begins, the world is alive with the joy of the Lord.

A Reality?

And yet it can all go so badly wrong! People get hassled by all the activity. The money runs short and there is worry. Someone gets sick and there is anxiety. Someone dear dies and there is heart-break. The family are away from home and there's emptiness. No one cares and there is great loneliness. So many people are selfish at this time and there is anger. It can be and often is a very difficult time for many people.

A Challenge

The challenge of the eight weeks is to set out to bring that joy to one another. For husbands and wives: plan the activities together and share in them as much as possible. For parents with families: involve the children of all ages as much as possible and encourage them to think of others as well as themselves. For children: set out to make this time very pleasant for parents and one another and plan how you can bring joy and happiness to some other people. For single people: involve yourselves with others in the celebration of this season and not just with people in need but people who can bring joy to you. For priests and religious: turn on the charm of God's love and brighten up the lives of those you live with and those you serve. For all: beware of selfishness, self-pity, self-preoccupation, anger. Practice forgiveness and smile a lot.

Features

The main feature of this time is that it is a spiritual season, celebrating the wonders of God's love for us. Prayer is vitally important. Confession is a great freedom. The Mass is a wonderful opportunity to bring that same joy to the community.

FIRST SUNDAY OF ADVENT

THEME
Our Salvation is near.

PRAYER FOCUS
Increase our strength of will for doing good.
Pray for the strength of will to do good. Ask the Lord now to
support you in your good works this week.

READINGS

1) Isaiah 2:1-5
Nation will not lift sword against nation.
Question: Do you ever lose heart because of
the bad state of the world? Why? When?

2) Response (to Psalm 121):
I rejoiced when I heard them say: 'Let us go to God's house.'
Repeat this response as often as you can this week.
Do you rejoice about going to God's house this week?

3) Romans 13:11-14
You must wake up now.
Question: What does this mean in your life?

4) Matthew 24:37-44
You too must stand ready.
Question: What do you specially need to do to be ready for the
coming of Christ?

QUESTIONS FOR ACTION
For Married Couples: In what ways have you settled down in
your love and taken each other for granted? Share this with one
another this week.

For Others: How will you bring joy to others this Christmas?

SECOND SUNDAY OF ADVENT

THEME
Prepare a way for the Lord.

PRAYER FOCUS
Open our hearts in welcome.
Pray for the gift of joy to welcome Jesus fully this Christmas.

READINGS

1) Isaiah 11:1-10
He does not judge by appearances
Question: In what ways do you judge by appearances?

2) Response (to Psalm 71)
In his days justice shall flourish and peace till the moon fails.
Repeat this response as often as you can this week.
Think of ways to bring justice and peace
to your family and community this week.

3) Romans 15:4-9
Everything was meant to teach us something about hope.
Question: What experiences in your life have given you a sense
of hope?

4) Matthew 3:1-12
Repent, for the kingdom of heaven is close at hand.
Question: In what ways do you need to repent?

QUESTIONS FOR ACTION
For Married Couples: Is there anything for which you need to ask
forgiveness from your wife/husband? Ask for that forgiveness
this week.

For Others: When did you last go to Confession? Will you go
this week in preparation for Christmas?

THIRD SUNDAY OF ADVENT

THEME
Joy in the Lord.

PRAYER FOCUS
May we experience the joy of salvation.
Christ came to save us. Pray that we can celebrate our salvation
this Christmas with love and thanksgiving.

READINGS

1) Isaiah 35:1-6; 10
Courage! Do not be afraid.
Question: How do you respond when God says to you 'Courage,
do not be afraid'?

2) Response (to Psalm 145)
Come, Lord, and save us.
Repeat this prayer as often as you can this week.
Do you really want to be saved?

3) James 5:7-10
Be patient until the Lord's coming. Do not lose heart.
Question: What makes it difficult for you to be Catholic?

4) Matthew 11:2-11
Happy the person who does not lose faith in me.
Question: What have been some of your most joyful memories
in the practice of your faith?

QUESTIONS FOR ACTION

For Married Couples: How could you bring joy to your
wife/husband in your love this week?
For Others: To whom could you bring special joy this week?

FOURTH SUNDAY OF ADVENT

THEME
God is with us.

PRAYER FOCUS
Fill our hearts with your love.
Pray that God will fill our hearts with his love this week.

READINGS

1) Isaiah 7:10-14
Ask the Lord your God for a sign ...
Question: Did you ever ask and receive a sign that confirmed
your faith? How did you react?

2) Response (to Psalm 23)
Let the Lord enter! He is the king of glory.
Repeat this prayer as often as possible this week.
Do you really let the Lord enter your life?

3) Romans 1:1-7
To you, who are called to be saints ...
Question: What does it mean to you to be called to be a saint?

4) Matthew 1:18-25
They will call him Emmanuel,
a name which means 'God-is-with-us'.
Question: How do you feel, knowing that God is with us?

QUESTIONS FOR ACTION:

For Married Couples: What plans do you have to spend time with
your wife/husband this week?

For Others: How could you bring a sense of the specialness of
Christmas to someone this week?

CHRISTMAS DAY

THEME
A Saviour is born for us.

PRAYER FOCUS
Bring us to eternal joy in the kingdom of heaven.
Pray that the eternal joy of Christmas birth
will be present in you, in your home and in the world today.

READINGS

1) Isaiah 9:2-7
You have made their gladness greater.
Question: What was your best experience of Christmas?

2) Response (to Psalm 95)
Today a saviour has been born to us; he is Christ the Lord.
Repeat this prayer as often as you can this week. Think especially
about what the birth of Christ means to you this Christmas.

3) Titus 2:11-14
Give up everything that does not lead to God.
Question: What could you 'give up' to bring you closer to God?

4) Luke 2:1-14
I bring you news of great joy,
a joy to be shared by the whole people.
Question: How will you share joy, a joy to be shared by the
whole people?

QUESTIONS FOR ACTION

For Married Couples: What gift (apart from the perfume and
socks!) do you think your wife/husband needs from you today?

For Others: Contact someone today whom you wouldn't normally contact on Christmas Day. Who will it be?

HOLY FAMILY
Sunday within the Octave of Christmas

THEME
Family life in the Lord.

PRAYER FOCUS
Help us to live united in respect and love.
Pray for peace and unity in your family this coming year.

READINGS

1) Ecclesiasticus 3:2-6; 12-14
The one who fears the Lord respects his/her parents.
Question: What do you most need to respect your parents for?

2) Response (to Psalm 127)
O blessed are those who fear the Lord and walk in his ways!
Repeat this prayer as often as you can this week.
Pray for the strength to live your life as the Lord wishes.

3) Colossians 3:12-21
Always be thankful.
Question: What are some of the things you are most grateful for
in your family?

4) Matthew 2:13-15; 19-23
Herod intends to search for the child and do away with him.
Question: What fears do you have for your loved ones?

QUESTIONS FOR ACTION

For Married Couples: What are the best qualities of each of your
children or the people closest to you? Tell them this week.

For Others: What are the nicest things about your mother/
father? Write these out this week and, if possible, tell them.

SECOND SUNDAY AFTER CHRISTMAS

THEME
Christ, the Wisdom of God.

PRAYER FOCUS
Show the nations the light of your truth.
Pray for the spread of God's truth in the world this year.

READINGS

1) Ecclesiasticus 24:1-4; 12-16
I have taken root in a privileged people.
Question: Do you feel privileged in belonging to the Church?

2) Response (to Psalm 147)
The Word was made flesh and lived among us.
Repeat this prayer in the Angelus every day this week.

3) Ephesians 1:3-6; 15-18
Before the world was made he chose us.
Question: Do you believe that God chose you?

4) John1:1-18
He came to his own domain
and his own people did not accept him.
Question: What does Christ ask that you find hard to do?

QUESTIONS FOR ACTION:

For Married Couples: What can you do to strengthen your marriage this year? Share this with your wife/husband.

For Others: What New Year's resolution will you make that would be helpful to your community?

BAPTISM OF THE LORD
Sunday after 6 January

THEME
Christ, the beloved of God.

PRAYER FOCUS
Keep us faithful to our calling.
Pray that you will be faithful to your Baptismal Promises.

READINGS

1) Isaiah 42:1-4; 6-7
Faithfully he brings true justice.
Question: Where do you see injustice in the world today? Are
there any ways in which you can bring true justice to these situ-
ations?

2) Response (to Psalm 28)
The Lord will bless his people with peace.
Repeat this prayer as often as you can this week. How will you
bring peace to your family or community this week?

3) Acts 10:34-38
Jesus Christ is Lord of all people.
Question: In what ways do you make Jesus the centre of your
life?

4) Matthew 3:13-17
'This is my Son, the Beloved; my favour rests on him.'
Question: When are you most proud of the faith that you have?

QUESTIONS FOR ACTION:

For Married Couples: Think of your wedding day when you said
yes to each other! How will you say yes to each other this week?

For Others: Think of a group that is working for justice. How
could you help that group this week?

Note

After the Baptism of the Lord, go to the Second Sunday of the Year and stay with the Sundays of the Year until Ash Wednesday. The number of Sundays of the Year which come before Lent varies from year to year, depending on the date of Easter. After Pentecost we return to Sundays of the Year.

2nd - 9th Sunday of the Year

Introduction

Now that the Christmas season is well and truly over many people heave a sigh of relief and, in the church as elsewhere, it can easily be 'Business as Usual'. But the Lord will not allow us to settle into dullness and mediocrity. The theme of this section is *hope* and the challenge is to practice hope, to build hope, to be filled with hope.

What is hope?

It can easily be seen as a vague kind of feeling that things might improve. Like most important things, hope is difficult to define. It is easier to describe. One of the main features of this gift of hope is enthusiasm – enthusiasm for being alive, for being in love, for the world in which we live, for the faith that has been given to us, enthusiasm for the love of God and his ways. All that doesn't just happen. It has to be worked at, practiced, chosen. Some people seem more naturally enthusiastic than others. Everyone can achieve it by entering fully into this time of Eucharist with Christ.

Enemies of hope

Many things can dampen down or even destroy this hope in our lives. For one thing, the weather at this time of the year knocks the heart out of some and brings on a kind of depression! The state of the world gets to many and causes them to despair. The state of the economy and the growing unemployment causes much anxiety – and closer to home as it were, the problems of relationships can get many people down, to the point where they wonder is it all worthwhile. What knocks the heart out of you? Whatever it is, it is an enemy of hope in your life.

Helps to hope

There is nothing we can do about the weather – except perhaps open ourselves up more fully to an appreciation of the wonders of creation and the movements of nature, and keep well covered! As regards everything else, our hope will never be destroyed in us in so far as we grow in a knowledge of the presence of the Lord with us. Through the Mass each week we are strengthened to face the problems of the world. Through the Word of God we are inspired to see things that are beyond immediate perception. By preparing well for Mass each Sunday we learn how to live in freedom and in truth where we can become even more con-cerned about the problems of the world at large and at home, but not be destroyed by them. With Christ we can face anything but we have to open ourselves more and more fully to his power of love.

In our close relationships hope is most fully restored and built up where there is a lot of praise and thanksgiving. During these weeks put a ban on all criticism and, anytime anyone is tempted to criticise, he/she should replace it with praise. During this time make a very special commitment to thank those closest to you in your life everyday for what they bring to you. In your marriage and family make these weeks a time of special affection in word and action. You will become much more enthusiastic! And it will help with the weather!

Some Features

In the readings the two main features are: a) the Second Readings almost all come from 1 Corinthians 1-4; b) the Gospel Readings mostly come from Matthew 4-5. Why not read those chapters to-gether and get the flow of God's Word? Then let it work on you as you prepare week by week.

SECOND SUNDAY OF THE YEAR

THEME
The Lamb of God.

PRAYER FOCUS
Show us the way to peace in the world.
Question: How much of a priority is that for you?

READINGS

1) Isaiah 49:3; 5-6
...so that my salvation may reach to the ends of the earth.
Question: Is that your ambition? What can you do about it?

2) Response (to Psalm 39)
Here I am Lord! I come to do your will.
Pray this until you can mean it from your heart.

3) 1 Corinthians 1:1-3
To those who are called to take their place among the saints.
Question: Do you see that as your call – to be a saint?

4) John 1:29-34
I am the witness that he is the Chosen one of God.
Question: How do you witness to Christ in your life?

QUESTIONS FOR ACTION

For Married Couples: How can you show your love for your
wife/husband in a special way this week?

For Others: Think of some missionary group. How could you
help them this week?

THIRD SUNDAY OF THE YEAR

THEME
Jesus, the light of the world.

PRAYER FOCUS
That our efforts may bring humankind to unity and peace.
Question: Do you think that is possible? Why?

READINGS

1) Isaiah 8: 23-9, 3
The people that walked in darkness has seen a great light.
Question: Where is 'the darkness' in our world today?

2) Response (to Psalm 26)
The Lord is my light and my help.
Pray this until you feel the strength of it.

3) 1 Corinthians 1:10-13; 17
I appeal to you to make up the differences between you.
Question: What divisions do you see in your community?

4) Matthew 4:12-23
Repent, for the kingdom of heaven is close at hand.
Question: In what ways do you see your community needs
repentance, to be different? In what ways do you need to change?

QUESTIONS FOR ACTION

For Married Couples: How could you bring a smile to the face of
your wife/husband this week?

For Others: Think of someone who is 'living in darkness'. How
can you be a light for them this week?

FOURTH SUNDAY OF THE YEAR

THEME
The way of the Lord.

PRAYER FOCUS
Help us to love you and all people as you love them.
Question: Is that desire the most important one of your life?

READINGS

1) Zephaniah 2:3; 3:12-13
Seek integrity, seek humility.
Question: How could you grow in these two virtues?

2) Response (to Psalm 145)
How happy are the poor in spirit;
theirs is the kingdom of heaven.
Pray this until you know the truth of it.

3) 1 Corinthians 1:26-31
If anyone wants to boast, let him boast about the Lord.
Question: Do you consider your faith your greatest treasure?
Why?/why not?

4) Matthew 5:1-12
Rejoice and be glad, for your reward will be great in heaven.
Question: In what ways is that promise important to you?

QUESTIONS FOR ACTION

For Married Couples: What are three of the nicest things about
your wife/husband at present? How will you tell her/him this
week?

For Others: Think of someone who is mourning at present. How
will you comfort them this week?

FIFTH SUNDAY OF THE YEAR

THEME
A light in the darkness.

PRAYER FOCUS
Keep us safe in your care.
Question: In what ways do you need God's protection?

READINGS

1) Isaiah 58:7-10
Share your bread with the hungry
and shelter the homeless poor.
Question: What is your reaction to that statement?

2) Response (to Psalm 111)
The good person is a light in the darkness for the upright.
Pray this until you want to be that light.

3) 1 Corinthians 2:1-4
Your faith should not depend on human philosophy
but on the power of God.
Question: How can you grow in that power of God?

4) Matthew 5:13-16
You are the salt of the earth. You are the light of the world.
Question: Is that too much to ask of people?

QUESTIONS FOR ACTION

For Married Couples: What special thing would you like your
wife/husband to do for you this week? Tell her/him.

For others: Think of some group that is working for the homeless. How could you help them this week?

SIXTH SUNDAY OF THE YEAR

THEME
The law of Christ – Love.

PRAYER FOCUS
Help us to live in your presence.
Question: What distracts you from the presence of God?

READINGS

1) *Ecclesiasticus 15:15-20*
To behave faithfully is within your power.
Question: In what areas of life do you find God's law most
difficult to live by?

2) *Response (to Psalm 118)*
They are happy who follow God's law.
Pray this until you know the truth of it.

3) *1 Corinthians 2:6-10*
Things that no eye has seen and no ear has heard.
Question: How important is the idea of heaven to you?

4) *Matthew 5:17-37*
I tell you, if your virtue goes no deeper than that of the Scribes
and Pharisees, you will never get into the kingdom of heaven.
Question: Do you see that you need to grow in holiness of life?
In what ways?

QUESTIONS FOR ACTION

For Married Couples: In what ways could you compliment your
wife/husband this week?

For Others: Think of someone with whom you haven't been in
touch recently. How will you contact that person in a special
way this week?

SEVENTH SUNDAY OF THE YEAR

THEME
The Lord is compassion and love.

PRAYER FOCUS
Help us to be like your Son in word and deed.
Question: What changes does that prayer call for in you?

READINGS

1) Leviticus 19:1-2; 17-18
You must not bear hatred in your heart.
Question: How does that statement affect you?

2) Response (to Psalm 102)
The Lord is compassion and love.
Pray this until you experience the warmth of it.

3) 1 Corinthians 3:16-23
Didn't you realise that you were God's temple?
Question: How do you need to grow in reverence and love for
your own body?

4) Matthew 5:38-48
Love your enemies and pray for those who persecute you.
Question: Who comes to mind for you when you hear
that statement of Christ?

QUESTIONS FOR ACTION

For Married Couples: How do you need to grow in reverence for
and freedom with your wife/husband physically and sexually?
How can you develop this in your relationship this week?

For Others: Think of some group that is engaged in
reconciliation of any kind. How can you help them this week?

EIGHTH SUNDAY OF THE YEAR

THEME
The God who cherishes us.

PRAYER FOCUS
Give us the joy and peace of serving you in freedom.
Question: Do you want these graces for yourself this week? If so,
how badly? If not, what blocks you?

READINGS

1) Isaiah 49:14-15
I will never forget you, says the Lord.
Question: How do you feel when you hear God say he is crazy
about you?

2) Response (to Psalm 61)
In God alone is my soul at rest.
Pray this response quietly until you are at peace.

3) 1 Corinthians 4:1-5
The Lord alone is my judge.
Question: What kind of judgement do you think the Lord
would make about you at present? Why?

4) Matthew 6:24-34
Do not worry about tomorrow.
Question: What worries about the future do you find it hard to
let go? How do these affect you?

QUESTIONS FOR ACTION

For Married Couples: What are two or three of the nicest things
about your wife/husband in recent times? How can you
acknowledge them this week?
For Others: Is there someone you know to be lonely or sad?
How could you reach out to them this week?

NINTH SUNDAY OF THE YEAR

THEME
Christ, our security.

PRAYER FOCUS
Keep us from danger and provide for all our needs.
Question: What dangers do you need the Lord to protect you
from?

READINGS

1) Deuteronomy 11, 18:26-28
See, I set before you today a blessing and a curse.
Question: How do you deal with choices that have to be made in
your life?

2) Response (to Psalm 30)
Be a rock of refuge for me, O Lord.
Pray this response, searching for your need for God.

3) Romans 3:21-25, 28
A person is justified by faith and not by doing something which
the Law tells her/him to do.
Question: What makes you feel good about yourself?

4) Matthew 7:21-27
The person who does the will of my Father in heaven
will enter the kingdom of heaven.
Question: What does this mean for you in your daily life?

QUESTIONS FOR ACTION

For Married Couples: When have you felt most secure in your
love for your wife/husband? Share those times this week.
For Others: Think of some group who are involved with disadvantaged people. How could you support them this week?

SECTION 3

Lent

Introduction

The big question that people ask as they approach Lent is: 'What am I going to give up?' It's another chance for smokers to try giving up cigarettes; for those who are worried about their drinking habits to give up drink; for the unfit to try jogging; for the children to learn all these bad habits of selfish self-denial!

'What am I going to give up for Lent?' is almost the right question. It could well be the second one. The first question for this season in preparation for Easter is: 'In what ways am I imprisoned so that I'm not totally free to love God with my whole heart and to love my neighbour as myself?' Then we can look at what we need to give up – or take up.

Freedom for what?

Some years ago a man who had served almost forty years in jail in America petitioned the authorities to let him stay for the rest of his life. He had got so used to where he was that he was frightened of the prospect of the world outside. So many people are like that. We can see it even in terms of physical health. The smoker who is so caught by nicotene that he/she risks cancer everytime a cigarette is lit. The alcoholic risks death for another drink. The overweight person risks a heart attack for another big meal, and so on. He/she needs to take charge of the situation and make a decision in favour of life, and this is possible as can be seen in the case of so many recovered alcoholics who resolutely follow the steps for recovery. They gain freedom to live, and it costs them.

Spiritually we are also so often imprisoned and because of that not free to live for God and for others – what Jesus refers to as the only true human living. We can be imprisoned by our own selfishness, self-centredness, self-preoccupation, sin. Lent is a time to look at these and gain freedom through repentance and penance.

We can be caught with our own busy-ness so that there is little or no time for what is most important in life. Lent is a time to look at this and gain freedom through prayer and through time given to those closest to us in marriage and family life. But it needs to be a time, both for prayer and for loved ones, that in some way may break the cycle of being overly busy with other things.

We can get imprisoned by our own possessions – there are never enough of them! Lent is a time for being generous with those in need, not just because they are in need but also so that through this generosity we might break the firm grip that possessions have on us. Our generosity needs to be significant.

We can be bound up by our emotions, especially by anger or resentment or anxiety or fear. Lent is a time to break this bond in us by forgiveness and letting go of the past and being ready to move ahead with Christ into the future.

An exciting time

Lent can be an exciting time for us if we enter into it in these ways that do not imply self-condemnation but that come from a vision of what we can be as people free to love, to hope, to trust, to dare, and that's what it should be for children also.

Some features

There is no particular progression in the Scripture readings during Lent this year. They are all urging us to change, not because we are evil but because the Lord is with us and he wants us to enter into full life with him. Work through these notes together week by week and great things will happen.

ASH WEDNESDAY

READINGS

1) Matthew 6:1-6; 16-18
Jesus said to his disciples:
i) When you give alms do not have it trumpeted before you.
ii) When you pray do not imitate the hypocrites.
iii) When you fast do not put on a gloomy face.

Questions: What are your commitments for Lent:
- to yourself, personally?
- to yourselves as a couple?
- to your family?
- to your community?

FIRST SUNDAY OF LENT

THEME
Christ, our new beginning.

PRAYER FOCUS
Help us to understand Christ's death and resurrection
and to reflect it in our lives.
Question: What does this prayer mean to you?

READINGS

1) Genesis 2:7-9; 3, 1-7
Did God really say you were not to eat
from any of the trees in the garden?
Question: What are some of your temptations in life?

2) Response (to Psalm 50)
Have mercy on us, O Lord, for we have sinned.
Pray this until you experience the truth of it.

3) Romans 5:12-19
Sin entered the world through one man, and through sin death.
Question: How real is sin to you?

4) Matthew 4:1-11
Jesus said: 'Be off, Satan!'
Question: How real is the devil to you? How real is Christ to you?

QUESTIONS FOR ACTION

For Married Couples: How could you recall and renew the start
of your love relationship this week?

For Others: Think of some group that is helping alcoholics to re-
cover. How could you be involved with that group this week?

SECOND SUNDAY OF LENT

THEME
It is wonderful for us to be here.

PRAYER FOCUS
Enlighten us with your word.
Question: How do you need more openess to the Scriptures?

READINGS

1) Genesis 12:1-4a
Leave your country, your family and your Father's house,
for the land I will show you.
Question: Do you ever find God very demanding of you?

2) Response (to Psalm 32)
May your love be upon us, O Lord,
as we place all our hope in you.
Pray this until you really want it to happen.

3) 2 Timothy 1:8-10
Bear the hardships for the sake of the good news.
Question: How do you handle things that are difficult
in life or in faith?

4) Matthew 17:1-9
'Lord, it is wonderful for us to be here.'
Question: When have you experienced joy like that?

QUESTIONS FOR ACTION

For Married Couples: What are three of the happiest memories
you have of your life together? How could you relive these this
week?

For Others: Think of some group that works for people who are
depressed. How could you help them this week?

THIRD SUNDAY OF LENT

THEME
Christ, the living water.

PRAYER FOCUS
Give us confidence in your love.
Question: What do you need for that to be answered?

READINGS

1) Exodus 17:3-7
'Is the Lord with us, or not?'
Question: Do you ever complain about God's seeming lack of
care? What happens?

2) Reponse (to Psalm 94)
O That today you would listen to his voice!
Harden not your hearts.
Pray this until you feel more open to God's word.

3) Romans 5:1-2; 5-8
This hope is not deceptive.
Question: When do you experience hope most fully?

4) John 4:5-42
These who worship must worship in spirit and truth.
Question: How much of your worship is from your heart and
how much is just formality?

QUESTIONS FOR ACTION:

For Married Couples: What is one of the nicest things that has
happened between you recently? How could you relive that
this week?

For Others: Think of some group that is dealing with drug
addiction. How could you assist them this week?

FOURTH SUNDAY OF LENT

THEME
He cares for us in our needs.

PRAYER FOCUS
Let us hasten towards Easter
with the eagerness of faith and love.
Question: What does that prayer mean to you?

READINGS

1) 1 Samuel 16:1; 6-7; 10-13
God does not see as man/woman sees; he looks at the heart.
Question: Is there anyone close to you whom you have written
off as no good? Why?

2) Response (to Psalm 22)
The Lord is my shepherd; there is nothing I shall want.
Pray this until you experience the gentleness of it.

3) Ephesians 5:8-14
Try to discover what the Lord wants of you.
Question: How can you do this?

4) John 9:1-41
Jesus saw a man who had been blind from birth. He cured him.
Question: What blind spots do you have about life and faith that
you need healed?

QUESTIONS FOR ACTION:

For married Couples: In what way do you most need your
wife/husband to love you at present? Tell her/him this week.

For Others: Think of some group who work for people with
physical disabilities. How can you help them this week?

FIFTH SUNDAY OF LENT

THEME
He raises to new life.

PRAYER FOCUS
Inspire us by his love, guide us by his example.
Question: In what ways do you need greater enthusiasm in your
faith?

READINGS

1) Ezekiel 37:12-14
I shall put my spirit in you, and you will live.
Question: In what ways do you see your community needs new
life?

2) Response (to Psalm 129)
With the Lord there is mercy and fullness of redemption.
Pray this until you experience the certainty of it.

3) Romans 8:8-11
Your interests are not in the unspiritual but in the spiritual.
Question: What are the main interests of your life?

4) John 11:1-45
If anyone believes in me, even though he dies he will live.
Question: What are your thoughts and feelings about death?

QUESTIONS FOR ACTION:

For Married Couples: In what special way could you surprise
your wife/husband this week?

For Others: Think of some group that helps to bring comfort to
the bereaved. How can you help them this week?

Holy Week - Easter Sunday

Introduction

The central reality of our faith as Christians is that Christ has risen from the dead and that he lives among us. Holy week is the celebration of Christ's journey into this new life, a journey that we are also invited to travel, knowing that he has gone before us and that he travels with us.

A difficult time

Holy Week is a difficult time for us. It is difficult because of the number of points of celebration. It is difficult because of the seriousness of the themes of betrayal and death. And it is difficult because people are becoming more and more busy in their ordinary lives and so don't have the time to enter into this occasion seriously.

It is important to make this week a special time of prayer and reflection. We do this at a community level by gathering in big numbers five times in the week. But we need to do it at a family level as well, and at a personal level also. This is the week when Lenten penance should be exercised in a special way by taking this time to journey with Jesus and so catch his Spirit.

Stages of the journey

1. Palm Sunday: From being celebrated to being forgotten.

2. Holy Thursday: From giving himself to his disciples in the Eucharist to being denied by them.

3. Good Friday: From surrendering himself to God's will to feeling abandoned even by God in death.

4. Holy Saturday: From complete emptiness in death to new life.

5. Easter Sunday: From the tomb to the ends of the earth.

During this Holy Week we journey through all these stages with Jesus so that he may bring us to new life and hope.

PALM SUNDAY

READINGS

1) Mark 11:1-10 or John 12:12-16

2) Isaiah 50:4-7

3) Response (to Psalm 21)
My God, My God why have you forsaken me.

4) Philippians 2:6-11

5) Mark 14:1-15, 49

A THOUGHT
The Crowds shouted:
(on Sunday) Hosanna! Blessings on him who comes in the name
of the Lord.
(on Friday) Crucify him! Crucify him!

QUESTIONS
Have you ever experienced the fickleness of other people?
Have you ever been guilty of it in relation to others, to Christ?

HOLY THURSDAY

READINGS

1) Exodus 12:1-8; 11-14

2) Response (to Psalm 115)
The blessing cup that we bless
is a communion with the blood of Christ.

3) 1 Corinthians 11:23-26

4) John 13:1-15

A THOUGHT
Jesus said: 'Do you understand what I have done to you?'

QUESTIONS
What is the closest you have ever felt to another person?
When have you felt closest to Christ?

GOOD FRIDAY

READINGS

1) Isaiah 52:13-53, 12

2) Response (to Psalm 30)
Father, into your hands I commend my spirit.

3) Hebrews 4:14-16; 5:7-9

4) John 18:1-19, 42

A THOUGHT
Jesus said: 'It is accomplished';
and bowing his head he gave up the spirit.

QUESTION
How do you feel when you think of the crucifixion of Jesus?

HOLY SATURDAY

READINGS

1) Genesis 1:1-2, 2

2) Genesis 22:1-18

3) Exodus 14:15-15:1

4) Isaiah 54:5-14

5) Isaiah 55:1-11

6) Baruch 3:9-15, 32:4-4

7) Ezechiel 36:16-17a; 18-28

NOTE
These seven readings from the Old Testament give a wonderful
insight into God's vision for our world and his providence in
leading us to his love.

A THOUGHT
'There is no need for alarm. He has risen, he is not here.'

QUESTION
How does your vision for the world need to grow
so as to become more like God's vision?

EASTER SUNDAY

THEME
Joy.

PRAYER FOCUS
Let our celebration today raise us up
and renew us by the Spirit that is within us.
Question: What could prevent you from being joyful today?

READINGS

1) Acts 10:34; 37-43
Now we are those witnesses.
Question: How does your life witness to Christ?

2) Response (to Psalm 117)
This day was made by the Lord; we rejoice and are glad.
Pray this response several times, to experience the joy of it.

3) Colossians 3:1-4
Let your thoughts be on heavenly things.
Question: What does this mean to you?

4) John 20:1-9
He saw and he believed.
Question: Why do you believe?

QUESTIONS FOR ACTION

For Married Couples: What is your greatest desire for your life
together? How can you work towards that this week?

For Others: To whom could you bring some happiness this
week?

Easter 2 - Pentecost

Introduction

Jesus Christ is risen from the dead. Alleluia! That's the confidence of our faith, the source of our hope, the inspiration for our love. What a great time of the year this is! Nature all around us is coming to new life. The colours are beginning to reappear. The smells are freshening again. The daylight is lengthening, life is good and our faith is renewed. It is a time for confidence and trust.

Confidence in what?

Our faith in Jesus Christ, our knowledge of him, our love for him can give us confidence in everything. First of all in ourselves: there are so many things that can weaken confidence in us, especially the poor self-image so many people carry around with them. Jesus walks with us enabling us to walk tall. Next it gives us confidence in our vocation whether religious, priest, single or married: especially today married couples can be shaken in their confidence because of so much break-up of marriages, so much talk about divorce, so much cynicism about the love of husbands and wives. Our faith calls on couples to take charge of their marriage relationship, work on it together, discover the great beauty and strength there is in their love, let that love shine out to change the world around them. So many marriages break down because couples let their life together drift so that there is nothing left to build on. It doesn't have to be like that.

Next, it gives us confidence in our family life: parents can easily be almost afraid of their children, not knowing how to deal with them. Your children are wonderful people, waiting for you to take the initiative with them, the initiative of love and humanity, of sharing the joys and struggles of life. Family life can be a wonderful experience if you only have confidence in yourselves and in your children.

Our faith gives us confidence in the church: Our church has many faults and always will have. We are a church of sinners. But the church is a marvellous people to belong to, especially if we get involved in building up the power that has been given by Christ. It's a time for confidence in the church, the people, and with that confidence proclaiming the love of God far and wide. Issues can divide us. Let Christ unite us so that we can hold up to the world the power of God's love.

Finally, it gives us confidence in the world around us. It is so easy to get depressed by the state of the world. But there are so many good and even great people out there all around us. If we set our sights on them and unite ourselves with them in the mission of making this world a better place, we will grow in confidence for the future of the world. God is at work all the time, in many ways, in every place, bringing good out of what is evil, creating salvation out of what seems to be almost lost.

Special features:

Over these next few Sundays we are offered the opportunity of growing in that kind of confidence as we walk with the risen Lord, listen to him, are inspired by him and open ourselves for a fresh outpouring of his Holy Spirit. The first reading from the Scripture for these Sundays is taken mostly from Acts 1-8; the second reading from 1 Peter 1-4; and the Gospel reading is from John 10-17 apart from John 20:19-31 and Luke 24:13-35. By making these chapters from the Scripture the basis of our thoughts and prayer during these weeks we will certainly catch the Spirit of confidence that God has in us, shown by giving us Jesus, our risen Lord.

SECOND SUNDAY OF EASTER

THEME
Easter Joy.

PRAYER FOCUS
Increase our awareness of your blessings
and renew your gift of life within us.
Question: What are some of the blessings in your life?

READINGS

1) Acts 2:42-47
The faithful all lived together
and owned everything in common.
Question: How do you react to that?

2) Response (to Psalm 117)
Give thanks to the Lord for he is good; for his love has no end.
Pray this until you can feel gratitude.

3) 1 Peter 1:3-9
You did not see him, yet you love him.
Question: What are the origins of your faith in Christ?

4) John 20:19-31
'Peace be with you.'
Question: In what ways do you need greater peace in your life?

QUESTIONS FOR ACTION

For Married Couples: What are some of the blessings of your life
together? Share these this week.

For Others: Think of some group that is working for peace.
How can you help them this week?

THIRD SUNDAY OF EASTER

THEME
Yes, it is true, the Lord is risen.

PRAYER FOCUS
May we look forward with hope to our resurrection.
Question: What do you need for this prayer to be answered?

READINGS

1) Acts 2:14; 22-28
My heart was glad and my tongue cried out with joy.
Question: Are you ever overcome with joy and happiness?

2) Response (to Psalm 15)
Show us, Lord, the path of life.
Pray this until you really want it.

3) 1 Peter 1:17-21
So that you would have faith and hope in God.
Question: What do you put your hope in for happiness?

4) Luke 24:13-35
'What matters are you discussing as you walk along?'
Question: What are some of your preoccupations in life?

QUESTIONS FOR ACTION

For Married Couples: How could you bring some extra
excitement to your marriage this week?

For Others: Think of some missionary group who work at
bringing faith and hope to others. How could you help them
this week?

FOURTH SUNDAY OF EASTER

THEME
Our way to New Life.

PRAYER FOCUS
Give us new strength and lead us to join the saints in heaven.
Question: In what ways do you need new strength in your faith?

READINGS

1) Acts 2:14; 36-41
'Save yourselves from this perverse generation.'
Question: How does that apply to us today?

2) Response (to Psalm 22)
The Lord is my shepherd; there is nothing I shall want.
Pray this until you can feel the strength in it.

3) 1 Peter 2:20-25
Through his wounds you have been healed.
Question: In what ways do you need healing in life?

4) John 10:1-10
I have come so that they may have life and have it to the full.
Question: What do you think of as a full life?

QUESTIONS FOR ACTION

For Married Couples: How could you bring a new freshness to
your marriage this week?

For Others: Think of some group whose work is for those who
have lost hope in any way. How can you help them this week?

FIFTH SUNDAY OF EASTER

THEME
Our Royal Priesthood.

PRAYER FOCUS
Give us true freedom.
Question: What limits your freedom of Spirit?

READINGS

1) Acts 6:1-7
The word of the Lord continued to spread.
Question: In what ways could you be more involved in the life of
the church?

2) Response (to Psalm 32)
May your love be upon us, O Lord,
as we place all our hope in you.
Pray this until you really want it.

3) 1 Peter 2:4-9
Set yourselves close to him so that you too
may be living stones making a spiritual house.
Question: What does that mean to you?

4) John 14:1-12
I am the way, the truth and the life.
Question: In what direction is your life going?

QUESTIONS FOR ACTION

For Married Couples: How could you show special affection for
your wife/husband this week?

For Others: Think of some group that is engaged in promoting
the environment. How can you help them this week?

SIXTH SUNDAY OF EASTER

THEME
The spirit of truth.

PRAYER FOCUS
Help us to celebrate our joy and to express in our lives
the love we celebrate.
Question: What prevents you from being more joyful at present?

READINGS

1) Acts 8:5-8; 14-17
As a result, there was great rejoicing in that town.
Question: What great things does your parish have to celebrate?

2) Response (to Psalm 65)
Cry out with joy to God all the earth.
Pray this until it comes from your heart.

3) 1 Peter 3:15-18
Have your answer ready for people who ask you
the reason for the hope you all have.
Question: What answer can you give for why you believe?

4) John 14:15-21
I shall ask the father, and he will give you the Spirit of truth.
Question: What does the Holy Spirit mean to you?

QUESTIONS FOR ACTION

For Married Couples: What are some of the nicest things that
have happened between you as husband/wife recently? Share
these this week.

For Others: Think of some group that works for justice. How
could you be involved with them this week?

SEVENTH SUNDAY OF EASTER

THEME
Jesus prays for us continually.

PRAYER FOCUS
Help us keep in mind that Christ lives with you and is with us.
Question: When have you experienced the presence of Christ?

READINGS

1) Acts 1:12-14
All joined in continuous prayer,
including Mary the Mother of Jesus.
Question: What does Mary mean to you in your life?

2) Response (to Psalm 26)
I am sure I shall see the Lord's goodness
in the land of the living.
Pray this until you experience the certainty of it.

3) 1 Peter 4:13-16
It is a blessing for you when they insult you
for bearing the name of Christ.
Question: Has that ever happened to you? How does it happen
today?

4) John 17:1-11
I pray for them; I am not praying for the world
but for those you have given me.
Question: How do you feel, knowing that Christ always prays
for you?

QUESTIONS FOR ACTION

For Married Couples: How could you pray for and with your
wife/husband this week?

For Others: Think of some group of contemplative people in the
church today. How could you be in touch with them this week?

PENTECOST SUNDAY

THEME
Receive the Holy Spirit.

PRAYER FOCUS
Let the Spirit continue to work in the world through us.
Question: How open are you to this prayer being answered?

READINGS

1) Acts 2:1-11
We hear them preaching in our own language
about the marvels of God.
Question: What are some of the best things about the church
today?

2) Response (to Psalm 103)
Send forth your Spirit, O Lord, and renew the face of the earth.
Pray this until you hunger for it to happen.

3) 1 Corinthians 12:3-7; 12-13
There is a variety of gifts but always the same Spirit.
Question: What are some of your best gifts? How do you use
them?

4) John 20:19-23
As the Father sent me, so I am sending you.
Question: Do you ever feel a sense of mission to your world?

QUESTIONS FOR ACTION

For Married Couples: How could you show your children how
much you love them this week?

For Others: Think of some group that is working for young
people. How could you help them this week?

Note

After Pentecost, go to Trinity Sunday. After that, you may have to go back into some of the later Sundays of section 2, depending on the date of Easter in this particular year. You then follow the sequence of the Sundays through until the end of the year.

Trinity Sunday - 15th Sunday of the Year

Introduction

The holidays are coming for a lot of people. Another few weeks and they'll be away. The preparations for the holidays can be exciting. But generally they can cause tension and frustration too. It's the time when so many men especially tend to leave all the details to their wives and then wonder why they're not being informed! It's a time when there can be a lot of 'martyrs' around, burdened by too much to do! People can often reach the time of holidays physically and emotionally drained with a lot of undercurrents that won't go away. These weeks should instead be a time of faith when together we can work to bring joy and contentment into each others' lives. What a great way then to begin the holidays.

A time of faith

When we are very busy, especially with a lot of details and a whole lot of different things to think about and get done, the first casualty very often is prayer. It's amazing how easily we let go of this power at the very times when we probably need it most. Through prayer we are put in touch with the reality of God and learn his presence and that reality opens us out then to see the things that are really important and distingush them from what is not really important. That's what faith is. It is a power to see things very differently and to live that new way in the company of the Lord. It is not really a very spiritualised thing at all.

Examples

1. Through faith, couples can see that the most important thing for them is their unity with one another. When that becomes

their aim then their actions are directed towards it. They plan together, work together, get over difficult moments together,
enjoy their time together. What a difference that would make
during these weeks!

2. Through faith, parents can see that nothing is as important for
their children as their time, attention, affection, understanding.
Parents could wear themselves out providing things for their
children during these weeks and yet not satisfy them because
they may not have experienced their parents' presence and love.

3. Through faith, we can all see the needs of the world around us
and not have to hide from or be destroyed by them. We are
opened up to contribute to those in need and to be part of the
community of the church which does not forget just because we
are looking after ourselves.

4. Through faith, we come to know our need for God and also
his presence. We get in touch with that God when we celebrate,
especially on the first Sunday of this series, the God of love, the
God who is Father, Son and Spirit. And we live with the assurance of his love, an assurance that makes life bright and beautiful even when it could be destroyed by darkness or pain.

Some features

This series of Sundays leads us from celebrating the God of love
into looking at how we need to change and grow so as to be able
to bring God's love more powerfully to our world. In the
Scripture Readings we are presented with the following pro-
gressions: a) the Second Readings are almost all from Romans 5-
8; b) the Gospel Readings are almost all from Matthew 9-13.
Why not read these chapters now at the beginning of this series
and catch some of the spirit of adventure that these Sundays can
be in your journey of faith?

TRINITY SUNDAY

THEME
The God of love.

PRAYER FOCUS
Help us to worship you by proclaiming
and living our faith in you.
Question: What do you need in order to have joy in your faith?

READINGS

1) Exodus 34:4-6; 8-9
'A God of tenderness and compassion, slow to anger,
rich in kindness and faithfulness.'
Question: Is that how you think about God?

2) Response (to Dan 3: 52-56)
To you glory and praise for ever more.
Pray this until you want it to happen.

3) 2 Corinthians 13:11-13
Be united; live in peace.
Question: How does peace need to grow in your family and
parish?

4) John 3:16-18
God loved the world so much that he gave his only Son.
Question: In what ways have you experienced God's love?

QUESTIONS FOR ACTION

For Married Couples: What have been some of the special times
in your married love recently? Share these this week.

For Others: Think of some group that works for building
community. How can you help them this week?

TENTH SUNDAY OF THE YEAR

THEME
The Lord is my light and my salvation.

PRAYER FOCUS
Teach us your truth and guide our actions in your way of peace.
Question: How open are you to learning and to changing?

READINGS

1) Hosea 6:2-6
What I want is love, not sacrifice.
Question: In what ways do you settle for less than is possible in
your relationships with God and with others?

2) Response (to Psalm 49)
I will show God's salvation to the upright.
Pray this as a statement of intent until you want to do it.

3) Romans 4:18-25
Your descendants will be as many as the stars.
Question: What are your hopes and/or your despairs about the
church today?

4) Matthew 9:9-13
Jesus said, 'I did not come to call the virtuous, but sinners.'
Question: How do you feel about Jesus' ease with sinners?

QUESTIONS FOR ACTION
For Married Couples: How could you surprise your wife/
husband in your love this week?
For Others: Is there anyone you need to forgive in your life?
How can you go about it this week?

ELEVENTH SUNDAY OF THE YEAR

THEME
Our calling.

PRAYER FOCUS
Help us to follow Christ and to live according to your will.
Question: What does 'God's Will' mean to you?

READINGS

1) Exodus 19:2-6
I will count you a kingdom of priests, a consecrated nation.
Question: Do you experience the specialness of having faith?

2) Response (to Psalm 99)
We are his people; the sheep of his flock.
Pray this until you know the specialness of it.

3) Romans 5:6-11
We were still helpless when Christ died for sinful people.
Question: What does this statement mean to you?

4) Matthew 9:36; 10:8
The harvest is great but the labourers are few.
Question: How could you develop a greater sense of urgency for
the world around you?

QUESTIONS FOR ACTION

For Married Couples: How could you heighten your sense of romance with each other this week?

For Others: Think of some group that is working for vocations
to religious life/priesthood. How could you encourage them
this week?

TWELFTH SUNDAY OF THE YEAR

THEME
Do not be afraid.

PRAYER FOCUS
Keep us always in your love.
Question: What do you need to trust God more fully?

READINGS

1) Jeremiah 20:10-13
He has delivered the souls of the needy
from the hands of evil people.
Question: Do you ever think that you may be wrong for trying to
live properly? When?

2) Response (to Psalm 68)
In your great love answer me, O Lord.
Pray this until you feel the security of it.

3) Romans 5:12-15
The gift considerably outweighed the fall.
Question: Do you ever fear for your salvation? Why?

4) Matthew 10:26-33
Do not be afraid of those who kill the body.
Question: What fears do you have in your life?

QUESTIONS FOR ACTION

For Married Couples: What fears do you have in your married
and family life? Share these with each other this week.

For Others: Think of some group that is promoting lay
missionary activity. How can you contribute to them this week?

THIRTEENTH SUNDAY OF THE YEAR

THEME
Welcoming Christ.

PRAYER FOCUS
Free us from darkness.
Question: How does this apply in your life?

READINGS

1) 2 Kings 4:8-11; 14-16
'What can be done for her then?', he asked.
Question: Has anyone been generous with you in your life?
Talk about them.

2) Response (to Psalm 88)
I will sing forever of your love, O Lord.
Pray this until you mean it.

3) Romans 6:3-4; 8-11
We believe that having died with Christ
we shall return to life with him.
Question: What does that mean to you?

4) Matthew 10:37-42
Anyone who welcomes you welcomes me.
Question: Do you believe this about yourself?

QUESTIONS FOR ACTION

For Married Couples: Plan a special day this week just to be
together. What would you personally like to do during it?

For Others: Think of some group that works at making
visitors/tourists welcome. How could you get involved with
them this week?

FOURTEENTH SUNDAY OF THE YEAR

THEME
Come to me and I will give you rest.

PRAYER FOCUS
Free us from sin.
Question: How do you need that prayer answered?

READINGS

1) Zechariah 9:9-10
Rejoice heart and soul, daughter of Zion.
Question: What's needed to make the church more joyful?

2) Response (to Psalm 144)
I will bless your name forever, O God my King.
Pray this until you feel the freedom of it.

3) Romans 8:9; 11-13
Your interests are not in the unspiritual but the spiritual.
Question: What are some of your preoccupations?

4) Matthew 11:25-30
Come to me and I will give you rest.
Question: In what ways are you burdened by life at present?

QUESTIONS FOR ACTION

For Married Couples: How do you need your wife/husband to love you and care for you during these Summer months? Share this this week.

For Others: Think of some group that provides holidays for children during the Summer. How can you help them this week?

FIFTEENTH SUNDAY OF THE YEAR

THEME
What kind of soil are we?

PRAYER FOCUS
May all who follow him reject what is contrary to the gospel.
Question: Do you want that prayer to be answered?

READINGS

1) Isaiah 55:10-11
The word that goes from my mouth does not return empty.
Question: How are you being fruitful for God?

2) Response (to Psalm 64)
Some seed fell into rich soil and produced its crop.
Pray this until you want it for yourself.

3) Romans 8:18-23
Creation still retains the hope of being freed.
Question: In what ways is the environment being destroyed?

4) Matthew 13:1-23
Others fell on rich soil and produced their crop.
Question: How do you need to change so as to become better
soil for the kingdom of God?

QUESTIONS FOR ACTION

For Married Couples: How could you speak your love for your
wife/husband this week?

For Others: Think of some group that is working for a better
Earth. How could you support them this week?

16th - 22nd Sunday
of the Year

Introduction

'Peace I leave you, my own peace I give you.'

These are some of the final words that Jesus spoke to his disciples and that he has left to us, the church. They express one of his most urgent desires for us and can be placed alongside his passionate prayer: 'Father may they be one'. It is a longing and desire that can take root in us at every level: between husbands and wives; parents and children; friends; neighbours; communities; nations. At times we can seem helpless in creating that peace in the last two of these – between communities and among nations. We are certainly not powerless in building peace in all the other areas of life.

What destroys peace?

The same elements that destroy peace can be found at every level of life. Firstly there is selfishness that is so strong in all of us. Because of selfishness we not only place our own needs ahead of those of others but very often have no concern for the needs of others as long as we ourselves are being satisfied. This can be seen clearly in many of the problems experienced by married couples and within families. Next, there are so many hurts from the past in people's lives that cause anger. These hurts do not necessarily come from the people we are living with but our anger is nonetheless poured out on them. Then again, there is the need in so many people to dominate others, to control others, to be in charge. This destroys peace because it creates a situation where there is a lot of fear and anxiety created. And injustice destroys peace. Whether that injustice is at an international or national level, or at the level of marriage and family relationships, the result is the same – people are abused by injustice and peace is not possible.

What builds peace?

Right now very many people are about to go on holidays or have already started them. A major key to those holidays being a success is the level of real peace that can be created and built. This is done firstly by being at peace with yourself. Leave the past behind at this point by asking for and giving forgiveness wherever that is necessary.

The experience of so many people is that the holidays are half-over before they unwind and the second half is spent in a growing anxiety about having to face it all again soon! What a terrible waste of wonderful opportunities.

Secondly, set out together to make these weeks really enjoyable for one another. That's the opposite to selfishness as we put each other's happiness as our priority. Personal happiness is then guaranteed.

Thirdly, create an atmosphere of joy and enjoyment. That is often the opposite to the atmosphere which is created by anger and in a setting of real enjoyment it is possible to see the mole-hills rather than imagine the mountains.

Fourthly, give each other a lot of space and personal freedom. This is the opposite of control and can lead to a real closeness to one another. The Summer can be a time of refreshment for us all and then we contribute to peace for the world.

Some features

The Second Readings for these Sundays are all taken from Romans 8-12; the Gospel Readings are all from Matthew 13-16. Why not make these part of your Summer reading?

SIXTEENTH SUNDAY OF THE YEAR

THEME
Our Merciful Judge.

PRAYER FOCUS
Fill us with your gifts.
Question: What particular gifts do you want now?

READINGS

1) Wisdom 12:13; 16-19
You are mild in judgement, you govern us with great lenience.
Question: Is that how you think about God?

2) Response (to Psalm 85)
O Lord, you are good and forgiving.
Pray this until you know the truth of it.

3) Romans 8:26-27
The Spirit comes to help us in our weakness.
Question: Do you find prayer easy/difficult? Why?

4) Matthew 13:24-43
Let them both grow till the harvest.
Question: Are you ever troubled about evil in the world?

QUESTIONS FOR ACTION

For Married Couples: What special surprise could you give your
wife/husband this week?

For Others: Think of some one who is housebound. How could
you help that person this week?

SEVENTEENTH SUNDAY OF THE YEAR

THEME
The treasure we have found.

PRAYER FOCUS
Help us use wisely the blessings you have given to the world.
Question: What are some of these blessings?

READINGS

1) 1 Kings 3:5; 7-12
Give me a heart to understand
how to discern between good and evil.
Question: What one thing would you most want from God?

2) Response (to Psalm 118)
Lord, how I love your law.
Pray this until you can mean it.

3) Romans 8:28-30
God co-operates with all those who love him.
Question: How do you experience the presence of God?

4) Matthew 13:44-52
He sells everthing he owns and buys the field.
Question: Is your faith your greatest treasure? Why/why not?

QUESTIONS FOR ACTION

For Married Couples: How important is your marriage to you?
Share this with each other this week.

For Others: Think of some group that works for mentally or
physically disadvantaged children. How could you help that
group this week?

EIGHTEENTH SUNDAY OF THE YEAR

THEME
The Lord who feeds us.

PRAYER FOCUS
Forgive our sins and restore us to life.
Question: How do you need that prayer answered?

READINGS

1) Isaiah 55:1-3
Pay attention, come to me; listen and your soul shall live.
Question: How real is God to you in daily life?

2) Response (to Psalm 144)
You open wide your hand, O Lord, you grant our desires.
Pray this until you experience the wonder of it.

3) Romans 8:35; 37-39
Nothing can come between us and the love of Christ.
Question: What distracts you most from a fuller relationship
with Christ?

4) Matthew 14:13-21
'Give them something to eat yourselves.'
Question: Do the problems of the world ever get you down?
What do you hear Christ ask of you at those times?

QUESTIONS FOR ACTION

For Married Couples: What special time will you give to each
other this week?

For Others: Think of some group that works for those suffering
from starvation in the world. How can you support that group
this week?

NINETEENTH SUNDAY OF THE YEAR

THEME
Courage! It is I.

PRAYER FOCUS
Increase your Spirit within us.
Question: What does that mean for your life?

READINGS

1) 1 Kings 19:9; 11-13
There was the sound of a gentle breeze.
Question: Do you ever make time for quiet prayer? When?

2) Response (to Psalm 84)
Let us see, O Lord, your mercy; and give us your saving help.
Pray this until you really want it.

3) Romans 9:1-5
I would willingly be condemned if it would help
my brothers/sisters.
Question: Do you ever feel deep sorrow when you see people
rejecting their faith?

4) Matthew 14:22-33
'Courage! It is I. Do not be afraid.'
Question: In what ways do you need healing from fear so that
you can be more courageous in life?

QUESTIONS FOR ACTION

For Married Couples: Do you ever feel taken for granted by your
wife/husband? Share this this week.

For Others: Think of some group that is working to help those
who are separated or divorced. How could you help that group
this week?

TWENTIETH SUNDAY OF THE YEAR

THEME
Mercy to every person.

PRAYER FOCUS
May we love you in all things and above all things.
Questions: How would that change your life?

READINGS

1) Isaiah 56:1; 6-7
My house will be called a house of prayer for all peoples.
Question: How conscious are you of how much the world needs
the power of God?

2) Response (to Psalm 66)
Let the people praise you, O God; let all the peoples praise you.
Pray this until it comes from your heart.

3) Romans 11:13-15; 29-32
God never takes back his gifts.
Question: What gifts of life could you use more fully?

4) Matthew 15:21-28
'Lord', she said, 'help me.'
Question: Have you ever experienced a very deep need for
God's help? What happened?

QUESTIONS FOR ACTIONS

For Married Couples: Is there anything for which you need to
forgive your wife/husband at present? Do it this week.
For Others: Think of some group that works for prisoners. How
could you help that group this week?

TWENTY-FIRST SUNDAY OF THE YEAR

THEME
On this rock I will build my Church.

PRAYER FOCUS
Make us one in mind and heart.
Question: What is needed for that prayer to be answered in your
community?

READINGS

1) Isaiah 22:19-23
Should he open, no one shall close;
should he close, no one shall open.
Question: What are some of your best/worst experiences of the
church?

2) Response (to Psalm 137)
Your love, O Lord, is eternal;
discard not the work of your hands.
Pray this until you experience the peace it brings.

3) Romans 11:33-36
All that exists comes from him.
Question: Do you ever experience the wonder of creation?

4) Matthew 16:13-20
'You are the Christ, the Son of the living God.'
Question: Is that the centre of your faith? What does it mean to
you?

QUESTIONS FOR ACTION

For Married Couples: What special surprise could you give your
wife/husband this week that would strengthen your love?

For Others: Think of some group that is working for the unity of
Christians. How could you support that group this week?

TWENTY-SECOND SUNDAY OF THE YEAR

THEME
The strength of Christ's Spirit.

PRAYER FOCUS
Increase our faith.
Question: What do you need for that to be answered?

READINGS

1) Jeremiah 20:7-9
There seemed to be a fire burning in my heart.
Question: Have you ever experienced that fire of faith/love?

2) Response (to Psalm 62)
For you my soul is thirsting, O Lord, my God.
Pray this until you can mean it.

3) Romans 12:1-2
Let your behaviour change, modelled by your new mind.
Question: What does this mean for you in your daily life?

4) Matthew 16:21-27
What will a man gain if he wins the whole world
and ruins his life?
Question: Why do so many people seem to do precisely that?

QUESTION FOR ACTION

For Married Couples: How could you arrange a special romantic
evening with each other this week?

For Others: Think of some group that promotes lay missionary
activity. How could you support and encourage that group this
week?

23rd - 28th Sunday of the Year

Introduction

This is the time when everything begins to get back to normal – back to work, back to school, back to the hum-drum of daily living. And the love of God and his word pursues us there also. This section of the church's year seems to draw us into the very heart of life – love. Like everything else, love can easily become ordinary, hum-drum, even a burden. It can lose its sparkle. This is a time especially to renew that sparkle and to bring our love alive.

Enemies of love

The most obvious enemy of love is hatred – a deep loathing of someone else. That is one that many of us don't normally have to do battle with. But there are many others that we do have to confront. Cynicism is probably the greatest. This can come from hurt, from disappointment, from being let down. It is expressed in a kind of hard, cold approach to life and especially to people who are close. A person can be very hard-working, dutiful, but sour. It is most often found in men but can also be present in women.

The most common enemy of love is taking each other for granted. People get used to one another and then fail to see and to acknowledge the beauty, the goodnesss, the generosity of one another. Love gets covered over with a cloud of despondency.

And then there is indifference. So often people are so preoccupied with their own lives, their own concerns that they are indifferent to what is happening to their own spouse or children. If asked, they will help. But they don't notice. How that affects the quality of love!

Unforgiveness is like a cancer in any relationship of love. There is so much to forgive each other for when people are living close to each other. When that forgiveness is not being given freely it eats away at the ability and even the desire to love.

Developing love

There are many different love relationships to be worked at and developed in life. These few weeks are a good time to work on them.

Firstly, there is the sexual love of husbands and wives. This is obviously much more than having sexual intercourse. It is about gaining and developing a true freedom with one another both physically and emotionally and personally. The great opportunity of marriage is for a man to really know what it's like to be a woman and yet to be even more a man; for a woman to know what it's like to be a man and so grow in her femininity. But not just any woman, any man – to know what it's like to be this woman, this man. This leads into great acceptance of one's own body/sexuality and freedom with each other's sexuality. It is a love that needs to be enjoyed.

Secondly, there is the affectionate love of parents with their children. We are becoming more aware of the terrible evil of child sex abuse, where children are used as objects of sexual pleasure, even at times by their parents. Children do need a lot of affection from their parents, an atmosphere where they can be relaxed, a relationship where they can be held and reassured, where they can laugh and cry. Parents need to take the initiative in this.

Thirdly there is the friendship love where we bring joy and happiness to those who are part of our lives as friends and family. This is built up through being in touch, being hospitable, being sensitive to the needs and affirming of the goodness of friends.

Fourthly there is the respectful love that is shown to the stranger, the casual acquaintance, the neighbour who is not necessarily a friend. This is developed by not interfering but always having a word of greeting, a smile, a helping hand ready for them.

Fifthly there is the all-pervading love of God that needs us to open ourselves to receive it and to return that love in all that we do. This love is developed especially through prayer in which we listen for all the wonderful things God has done for us and through which we commit ourselves to loving him.

Some features

Most of the prayers of the Sunday Masses during this time are begging for a greater openness to God's love and a real commitment in our love for one another. Let that be the centre of your prayer right through this time.

The second Reading for most of these Sundays is from Philippians 1-4; The Gospel Readings are all from Matthew 18-22. Why not read through these chapters and catch the flavour of what is being offered to us in the weeks ahead?

TWENTY-THIRD SUNDAY OF THE YEAR

THEME
Power given to us, the church.

PRAYER FOCUS
Give us true freedom.
Question: In what ways do you need this prayer answered?

READINGS

1) Ezechiel 33:7-9
Warn them in my name.
Question: How do you feel about standing up for what is right?

2) Response (to Psalm 94)
O that today you would listen to his voice!
Harden not your hearts.
Pray this until you experience freedom of heart.

3) Romans 13:8-10
You must love your neighbour as yourself.
Question: What are the implications of that for your life?

4) Matthew 18:15-20
Where two or three meet in my name,
I shall be there with them.
Question: Do you believe this promise of Christ?
What difference does it make in your life?

QUESTIONS FOR ACTION

For Married Couples: How could you grow in freedom with each
other? Share this this week.

For Others: Think of some group that is working for marriage
and family life. How could you help this group this week?

TWENTY-FOURTH SUNDAY OF THE YEAR

THEME
Forgive always.

PRAYER FOCUS
May we serve you with all our heart.
Question: How do you need this prayer answered?

READINGS

1) Ecclesiasticus 27:30-28:7
Resentment and anger, these are foul things.
*Question:*When have you felt resentment and anger in your life?
How have you handled them?

2) Response (to Psalm 102)
The Lord is compassion and love,
slow to anger and rich in mercy.
Pray this until you experience the Lord's presence

3) Romans 14:7-9
The life and death of each of us has its influences on others.
Question: In what circumstances do you find forgiveness
difficult?

QUESTION FOR ACTION

For Married Couples: Is there anyone in your husband/wife's life
that you need to forgive? How will you do it this week?

For Others: Is there anyone in your life towards whom you have
a grudge or anger? What will you do about it this week?

TWENTY-FIFTH SUNDAY OF THE YEAR

THEME
The generous love of God.

PRAYER FOCUS
May we love one another.
Question: What do you need so that you could really want that
prayer answered urgently?

READINGS

1) Isaiah 55:6-9
Seek the Lord while he is still to be found.
Question: How urgent is your desire for a deeper relationship
with God?

2) Response (to Psalm 144)
The Lord is close to all who call him.
Pray this until you experience the gentleness of it.

3) Philippians 1:20-24; 27
Life to me is Christ.
Question: What does that mean to you in your life?

4) Matthew 20:1-16
Why be envious because I am generous?
Question: Do you ever resent God's love for others?

QUESTIONS FOR ACTION

For Married Couples: What gift could you give your wife/
husband this week?

For Others: Think of some group that works for the starving of
the world. How could you be generous with that group this
week?

TWENTY-SIXTH SUNDAY OF THE YEAR

THEME
The power of truth.

PRAYER FOCUS
Continue to fill us with your gifts of love.
Question: What are some of your best qualities? How do you use
them for others?

READINGS

1) Ezechiel 18:25-28
'You object, what the Lord does is unjust!'
Question: Do you ever think you could do a better job than God?

2) Response (to Psalm 24)
Remember your mercy, Lord.
Pray this until you want it for the whole world.

3) Philippians 2:1-11
Always consider the other person to be better than yourself.
Question: Do you think this is possible? Would you want it?

4) Matthew 21:28-32
Tax collectors and prostitutes
are making their way into heaven before you.
Question: This was addressed to very good people. What does it
say to you?

QUESTIONS FOR ACTION

For Married Couples: How can you grow in your sexual love this
week?

For Others: Think of some group that is working for prisoners of
conscience. How can you support the group this week?

TWENTY-SEVENTH SUNDAY OF THE YEAR

THEME
They will respect my son.

PRAYER FOCUS
Keep us in your peace.
Question: What do you need in order to be more peaceful
at present?

READINGS

1) Isaiah 5:1-7
Why did it yield sour grapes instead?
Question: In what ways do we, the church, deserve
that condemnation today?

2) Response (to Psalm 79)
The vineyard of the Lord is the house of Israel.
Pray this until you catch the spirit of it.

3) Philippians 4:6-9
The God of peace will be with you.
Question: Do you ever experience the peace that God's love
brings? When?

4) Matthew 21:33-43
It was the stone rejected by the builders
that became the keystone.
Question: How do you see Jesus being rejected today?

QUESTIONS FOR ACTION

For Married Couples: How could you surprise your wife/hus-
band in your love this week?

For Others: Think of some group that is working for the renewal
of the church. How could you support that group this week?

TWENTY-EIGHTH SUNDAY OF THE YEAR

THEME
Many are called but few are chosen.

PRAYER FOCUS
May our love for you express itself in our eagerness
to do good for others.
Question: What do you need for that prayer to be answered?

READINGS

1) Isaiah 25:6-10
The Lord is the one in whom we hoped.
Question: Where do you place your hope for life?

2) Response (to Psalm 22)
In the Lord's own house shall I dwell for ever and ever.
Pray this until you want it from your heart.

3) Philippians 4:12-14; 19-20
There is nothing I cannot master
with the help of the one who gives me strength.
Question: Is that your experience of faith? Why/why not?

4) Matthew 22:1-14
Everything is ready. Come to the wedding.
Question: Why do many seem to refuse that invitation?

QUESTIONS FOR ACTION

For Married Couples: In what way would you like to see your
marriage grow in the months and years ahead? Share that this
week.

For Others: Think of some group that is working with young
people in the church. How could you help that group this
week?

29th Sunday -
Christ the King

Introduction

With this section of the church's liturgy we come to the end of another year in our journey of faith. I hope it has been a good year for you and that you found these notes helpful in finding God's ways for life more fully.

At this time of year the nights begin to close in quickly, the temperature drops and there's need for heavier clothing; nature takes on a certain bleakness. All of this can tend to force us to look inwards and to withdraw into ourselves.

Towards the end of the year, either calendar or church, we can be inclined to look back at what has happened or not happened. Sometimes what we see there gives us joy and comfort. Some of what we see might fill us with regret or anger or self-blame.

Faith teaches us to keep looking ahead, to see all the wonderful possibilities that are there for us in God's love for us and our love for one another. That is why the theme 'ambition' has been chosen for these few weeks. St Paul writes 'Be ambitious for the higher gifts' and then places love at the top of all of those. That's where we need to place it also.

Some questions

1. What is your ambition for your own life in the year ahead? Maybe that seems like a strange question to you but it could be a very important one. What would you like to have accomplished by this time next year? So many people just drift along year by year and are simply surprised at so much that happens – sometimes surprised to find themselves alive! Life will always hold surprises but they are the more enjoyable when we are going somewhere. Where are you going? Is it leading to eternal life? Is that anywhere in your ambitions or is it just a vague hope for you?

2. What is your ambition for marriage in the year ahead? The marriage relationship stays very alive when husband and wife are working together to make it happen. But you can only work at a marriage when you are going somewhere with it. So many couples simply settle down and get into a rut. It becomes dull and dreary rather than being wonderful and strong. Where do you as a couple want your marriage to be this time next year? How will you work at bringing it there?

3. What are your ambitions for your children in the next year? Parents always want what is best for their children and it pains them when they are not able to give them as much as they want. That pain will be experienced by many parents in the next few months if they cannot give what their children want for Christmas, or maybe cannot give as much as the parents of their children's friends give to them. But are your ambitions purely centred on material things, on success, on advancement?

How much of your ambition is focused on wanting your children to grow and live in freedom, in joy, in the security of knowing how much they are loved, in the peace of knowing they are accepted and forgiven and admired? That ambition might mean a few changes with your time, your attention, your ability to show love.

4. What is your ambition for the church in the year ahead? Another strange question, maybe! But it is one that laity need to learn to ask and to grow in. The church has been given so much power for the world. It remains unused because we don't have ambitions for setting it free. What would you like your parish to be like this time next year? How can you contribute to bringing it to that point?

5. What is your ambition for our world in the year ahead? At Christmas and the New Year Our Holy Father, among many world leaders, will express his hopes and dreams for the next year. What are yours? How would you like to see the world in twelve months' time? What can/will you do about it in order to bring that dream at least some of the way to reality?

It is easy to have vague hopes about things. This generally shows when we spend our time blaming others and even God for the way things are. When we develop ambitions in all these areas we are immediately involved and it's in that involvement that we experience life to the full.

Some features

The two main features of the Scripture Readings during these next few Sundays are a) the Second Readings are almost all from 1 Thessalonians 1-5; b) the Gospel Readings are all from Matthew 22-25. It can be a very helpful thing to read these chapters through so as to catch the flow of the Scriptures. And then week by week travel that journey from preoccupation with your concerns to the wonderful knowledge that Jesus is Lord, our King of love.

TWENTY-NINTH SUNDAY OF THE YEAR

THEME
Give to God what belongs to God.

PRAYER FOCUS
Give us strength and joy in serving you as followers of Christ.
Question: How do you need that prayer answered?

READINGS

1) Isaiah 45:1; 4-6
Though you do not know me, I arm you.
Question: How do you cope with uncertainty in your faith?

2) Response (to Psalm 95)
Give the Lord glory and power.
Pray this until you really want it.

3) 1 Thessalonians 1:1-5
We always mention you in our prayers
and thank God for you all.
*Question:*You are always being prayed for.
How does that affect you?

4) Matthew 22:15-21
Give back to Caesar what belongs to Caesar –
and to God what belongs to God.
Question: In what ways do you see people are hypocritical about
their religion? Are you?

QUESTIONS FOR ACTION

For Married Couples: What do you appreciate most about your
wife/husband? How could you tell her/him this week?

For Others: Think of some group that works for justice in the
world. How could you support that group this week?

THIRTIETH SUNDAY OF THE YEAR

THEME
The Greatest Commandment.

PRAYER FOCUS
May we do with loving hearts what you ask of us.
Question: What does that prayer mean to you?

READINGS

1) Exodus 22:20-26
If he (the poor) cries to me I will listen, for I am full of pity.
Question: What kinds of injustices do you see in society today?

2) Response (to Psalm 17)
I love you, Lord, my strength.
Pray this until you experience that love.

3) 1 Thessalonians 1:5-10
You broke from idolatry when you were converted to God.
Question: What kinds of idolatry exist in our world today? Is
there any idolatry in your life?

4) Matthew 22:34-40
Master, which is the greatest commandment of the Law?
Question: Do you really want to learn what is most important in
life?

QUESTIONS FOR ACTION

For Married Couples: How do you need to change so as to put
your wife/husband number one in your priorities? Share this
this week.

For Others: Think of some group that is working for renewal in
the church. How could you support them this week?

THIRTY-FIRST SUNDAY OF THE YEAR

THEME
Practise what you preach.

PRAYER FOCUS
May we live the faith we profess and
trust your promise of eternal life.
Question: What do you need in order to answer this prayer?

READINGS

1) Malachi 1:14-2:2, 8-10
Priests, this warning is for you.
Question: What is your attitude to the priests who serve you?
How should these attitudes change?

2) Response (to Psalm 130)
Guard my soul in peace before you, O Lord.
Pray this response, and let it take place.

3) 1 Thessalonians 2:7-9, 13
It (the faith) is still a living power among you.
Question: In what ways do you need to be more positive about
your parish community?

4) Matthew 23:1-12
The greatest among you must be your servant.
Question: Where do you see hypocrisy in yourself and in the
Church around you?

QUESTIONS FOR ACTION
For Married Couples: Plan a romantic evening together this week.
For Others: How could you reach out to someone who has given
up going to Mass?

THIRTY-SECOND SUNDAY OF THE YEAR

THEME
Stay Awake.

PRAYER FOCUS
Give us freedom of spirit and health in mind and body.
Question: In what ways do you need that prayer answered?

READINGS

1) Wisdom 6:12-16
Wisdom is bright and does not grow dim.
Question: Do you ever take quiet time for thinking and praying?

2) Response (to Psalm 62)
For you my soul is thirsting, O God, my God.
Do you mean this? Pray the response until you can mean it.

3) 1 Thessalonians 4:13-18
We want you to be quite certain about those who have died.
Question: Have you every experienced a loved one dying?
How has it, or the knowledge of death, changed you?

4) Matthew 25:1-13
Stay awake, because you do not know either the day or hour.
Question: What are your priorities in life at present?

QUESTIONS FOR ACTION

For Married Couples: How could you be more attentive to the
needs of your wife/husband this week?

For Others: Think of some group that is working for adult
education in the faith. How could you support and encourage
them this week?

THIRTY-THIRD SUNDAY OF THE YEAR

THEME
Trust in Christ.

PRAYER FOCUS
Keep us faithful in serving you.
Question: What does that prayer mean to you?

READINGS

1) Proverbs 31:10-13; 19-20; 30-31
A perfect wife – who can find her?
Question: In what ways do you find sexist attitudes in yourself
and others?

2) Response (to Psalm 127)
Blessed are those who fear the Lord.
Pray this until you feel the power in it.

3) 1 Thessalonians 5:1-6
We do not belong to the night or to the darkness.
Question: How do you need to grow in confidence in life?

4) Matthew 25:14-30
You have been faithful in small things,
I will trust you with greater.
Question: How willing are you to be more involved with
Christ?

QUESTIONS FOR ACTION

For Married Couples: In what ways do you need greater
freedom about your sexuality in your relationship with your
wife/husband? Share this this week.

For Others: Think of some group that is working for equality for
women in society and in the church. How could you help them
this week?

LAST SUNDAY OF THE YEAR

THEME
Christ the King.

PRAYER FOCUS
May all in heaven and earth acclaim your glory
and never cease to praise you.
Question: What do you need to be joyful at present?

READINGS

1) Ezechiel 34:1 1-12; 15-17
I myself will pasture my sheep.
Question: When have you ever experienced the love of Christ?

2) Response (to Psalm 22)
The Lord is my shepherd; there is nothing I shall want.
Pray this until you experience the consolation of it.

3) 1 Corinthians 15:20-26; 28
So that God may be all in all.
Question: How do you need to grow so that this desire becomes
your own?

4) Matthew 25:31-46
In so far as you did this to one of the least of these
brother/sisters of mine, you did it to me.
Question: Do you believe that what you do to others is how you
practice your faith?

QUESTIONS FOR ACTION

For Married Couples: How can you make this week joyful for
each other?

For Others: Think of some group that is working for the homeless and destitute. How can you help that group this week?

Year B

Advent 1 - The Baptism of the Lord

Introduction

The great effort of human life is to search for more. Many people would not identify this as a search for God and yet that is precisely what it is. The human heart can not be satisfied except by God and his love. And yet he remains so hidden. Even for people of faith God is not seen a lot of the time. Faith does not give us vision but rather a direction in which to look so that we can catch glimpses of the God who loves us so much and is always close to us.

Advent

During the four weeks of Advent we celebrate our God hidden in Mary's womb. Pregnancy is a wonderful, mysterious, awesome event in human life. It is a silent event, and it's into that silence of Mary's womb that God enters. It is there that he is still to be found – in all the silent, mysterious things of life. Advent is a time of waiting, a time of listening for that God who is so close to us and yet not seen.

Christmas

The hidden God reveals himself in the most unexpected way – in a baby born in total poverty, in a place where no one should have ever heard about it and yet everyone has. We celebrate this extraordinary love of God now, not just as a past event but as happening among us, in the same ways God is still being born among us. In Christ he is still sending his angels, he is still gathering us to rejoice like the shepherds, he is still prompting people to search for him and find him like the Maji, in spite of so much evil in the world.

Baptism of the Lord

Jesus' Mission in the world was to reveal our hidden God as the God who loves us with an infinite love. This section leads us up to that mission being revealed at his Baptism. It is only in Christ that we can know the hidden God and enter into his hiding place. At this time we celebrate that faith. We also begin again taking on our mission as the Church which is the same as that of Jesus – to bring the world into the hiding place of God and in there, in our own hearts, to know his wonderful love.

FIRST SUNDAY OF ADVENT

THEME
Waiting for God

PRAYER FOCUS
That Christ may find an eager welcome at his coming
Question: Recall times when you eagerly awaited some one or
something. What was your welcome like?

READINGS

1) Isaiah 63:16-17; 64, 1; 3-8
Lord, you are our Father; we the clay, you the Potter.
Question: Can you think of one thing in your life that you would
like God (the Potter) to change and re-mould this Advent?

2) Response (to Psalm 79)
God of hosts, bring us back; let your face shine on us
and we shall be saved.
Pray this response thinking about what you need help with at
this time.

3) 1 Corinthians 1:3-9
I thank God that you have been enriched in so many ways.
Question: In what ways has God enriched your life?

4) Mark 13:33-37
Jesus said: Stay awake!
Question: What words come to mind when you think of
Christmas'? What can you do this Advent to prepare for
Christ's coming at Christmas?

QUESTIONS FOR ACTION

For Married Couples: Before the busyness and rush of Christmas
arrives take time to plan a romantic time together. Perhaps you
could plan something for each week of Advent to enhance your
romance.

For Others: Thank someone who has enriched your life. When
making your card list, include people who might get very few
greetings.

SECOND SUNDAY OF ADVENT

THEME
The Good News

PRAYER FOCUS
Remove the things that hinder us
from receiving Christ with joy.
Question: What prevents you from receiving Christ with joy?

READINGS

1) Isaiah 40:1-5, 9-11
A voice cries: 'Prepare in the wilderness a way for the Lord'
Question: What helps me to prepare for the Coming of Christ at
Christmas?

2) Response (to Psalm 84)
Let us see, O Lord, your mercy and give us your saving help.
Pray this response this week for justice and peace in Ireland.

3) Peter 3:8-14
What we are waiting for is what he promised:
the new heavens and new earth.
Question: How do you feel about God promising us a new heaven
and a new earth? What will they be like?

4) Mark 1:1-8
John the Baptist appeared proclaiming a baptism
of repentance for the forgiveness of sins.
Question: What plans have you for going to Confession this
Advent? Do you see it as an important part of your preparation
for Christmas?

QUESTIONS FOR ACTION

For Married Couples: What special surprise could you give your
wife/husband this week to bring joy to each other?

For Others: Plan to set aside some of your Christmas spending
money for someone in need to bring joy to them.

THIRD SUNDAY OF ADVENT

THEME
Our joy in Christ.

PRAYER FOCUS
May we, your people, experience the joy of salvation.
Question: What does this mean for you?

READINGS

1) Isaiah 61:1-2; 10-11
He has sent me to bring good news to the poor,
to bind up hearts that are broken.
Question: To whom do you see this Scripture referring? Are you
to bring the Good News to those at home, outside in the parish
or wider afield?

2) Response (to Magnificat)
My soul rejoices in my God.
Repeat this response as a prayer of praise, joy and thanks for all
that God has accomplished through Mary.

3) 1 Thessalonians 5:16-24
Be happy at all times.
Question: What makes you happy? Make a list of things that
make you happy. Thank God for them.

4) John 1:6-8; 19-28
He (John the Baptist) was not the light, only a witness
to speak for the light.
Question: We are called to witness to Christ – how can you do
that in your life now?

QUESTIONS FOR ACTION

For Married Couples: Light a candle as a symbol of the light of Christ
that your marriage is to others. How can you bring joy to each
other this week? Plan to do at least one thing to bring this joy.

For others: Whom do you know has little joy in their lives? Plan
to bring them a little joy this week.

FOURTH SUNDAY OF ADVENT

THEME
Mary, the ark of God's Covenant.

PRAYER FOCUS
Lord, fill our hearts with your love.
Question: Think of some loving things you did and experienced
last week. Can you thank God for the goodness in yourself and
others?

READINGS

1) 2 Samuel 7:1-5; 8-11; 16
The Lord will make you great.
Question: What in your life is holding you back from being
great?

2) Response (to Psalm 88)
I will sing forever of your love, O Lord.
As you pray this response this week,
reflect on the Lord's continuing love for you.

3) Romans 16:25-27
The Good News' must be broadcast to pagans everywhere
to bring them to the obedience of faith.
Question: What pagan values do you see around us at this time
that block out the true meaning of Christmas?

4) Luke 1:26-28
Rejoice so highly favoured. The Lord is with you.
Question: Reflect on the Annunciation – how much is Mary part
of your faith?

QUESTIONS FOR ACTION

For Married Couples: Mary said 'yes' let it be. Decide on ways of
saying 'yes' to each other this week.

For Others: Pray for those who have sent Christmas greetings.
Visit a single parent this week, spend some time or offer help if
needed.

CHRISTMAS DAY

THEME
The Word was made flesh.

PRAYER FOCUS
He shared our weakness; may we share his glory.
Question: What do you need to be more enthusiastic about life at
present?

READINGS

1) Isaiah 52:7-10
All the ends of the earth shall see the salvation of our God.
Question: How can you make Christmas Day full of life and joy
for those around you?

2) Response (to Psalm 97)
All the ends of the earth have seen the salvation of our God.
Pray this for some time, thinking of various parts of the world.

3) Hebrews 1:1-6
Let all the angels of God worship him.
Question: How much do you take Christmas for granted?

4) John 1:1-18
The Word was made flesh; he lived among us.
Question: Have you ever felt really loved by God? When ? How?

QUESTIONS FOR ACTION
For Married Couples: When were you happiest about your
relationship in the last year? Share this with your wife/husband
today.
For Others: Is there someone you could visit or phone today and
who would be surprised and glad to hear from you?

HOLY FAMILY

THEME
The Holy Family.

PRAYER FOCUS
Help us to live as the Holy Family, united in respect and love.
Question: How do you feel when your family or community are
united in respect and love?

READINGS

1) *Ecclesiasticus 3:2-6; 12-14*
Long life comes to him who honours his father, he who sets
his mother at ease is showing obedience to the Lord.
Question: Which qualities in your mother and father do you
especially remember?

2) *Response (to Psalm 127)*
O blessed are those who fear the Lord and walk in his ways.
Pray this response for your parents and all parents today.

3) *Colossians 3:12-21*
Wives, give way to your husbands, as you should in the Lord.
Husbands, love your wives and treat them with gentleness.
Question: What do you think St Paul is asking of wives and
husbands? Is it relevant for us today?

4) *Luke 2:22-40*
The child grew to maturity, and he was filled with wisdom.
Question: What qualities and example do you think did Joseph
and Mary display in order to help Jesus grow to maturity and
be filled with wisdom?

QUESTIONS FOR ACTION
For Married Couples: What do you like best about your wife as a
mother, your husband as a father? Write down a list and share
it with each other.

For Others: What are the things you like best about your mother,
father? Let them know that, if possible.

SECOND SUNDAY AFTER CHRISTMAS

THEME
Christ, the wisdom of God

PRAYER FOCUS
Fill the world with your splendour

READINGS

1) Sirach 24:1-4; 12-16
I have taken root in a privileged people.
Question: What does this mean to you? How might this
knowledge affect your life?

2) Response (to Psalm 147)
The word was made flesh and lived among us.
Repeat this prayer in the Angelus each day.
Where do you see Jesus among us today?

3) Ephesians 1:3-6; 15-18
May he enlighten the eyes of your mind so that you can see
the hope his call holds for you.
Question: What kind of person do you think Christ is calling you
to be? Does this knowledge fill you with hope?

4) John 1:1-18
The word was the true light that enlightens all men and women.
Question: Is Jesus the true light and the centre of your life? If not,
what keeps you from making him the centre of your life?

QUESTIONS FOR ACTION

For Married Couples: Ask each other – 'In what way could I bring
you a sense of hope this coming year?' Begin now to act on the
answer.

For Others: What New Year's resolution could you make that
would be helpful to the Parish/Community?

BAPTISM OF THE LORD

THEME
The Baptism of Jesus.

PRAYER FOCUS
Keep us faithful to our calling.
Question: As a Christian what do you understand this to mean?

READINGS

1) Isaiah 42:1-4; 6-7
I have endowed him with my spirit
that he may bring true justice to the nations.
Question: Which groups of people do you think are unjustly
treated in our community? Is there anything positive you can
do about this?

2) Response (to Psalm 28)
The Lord will bless his people with peace.
With complete trust in the Lord pray this response for peace in
our homes, country and world.

3) Acts 10:34-38
Jesus went about doing good and curing all who had
fallen into the power of the devil.
Question: In which areas of your life do you need the Lord's
healing, e.g.\ someone you can't forgive, some hurt you're
carrying? Ask the Lord for healing this week.

4) Mark 1:7-11
I have baptised you with water, but he will baptise you
with the Holy Spirit.
Question: What special gifts of the Spirit do you think you have?

QUESTIONS FOR ACTION

For Married Couples: What does your marriage mean to you?
Give a small gift if possible as a symbol of this.

For Others: Pray for or visit or write to your Godparents this
week.

Note

After the Baptism of the Lord, go to the Second Sunday of the Year and stay with the Sundays of the Year until Ash Wednesday. The number of Sundays of the Year which come before Lent varies from year to year, depending on the date of Easter. After Pentecost we return to Sundays of the Year.

2nd - 9th Sunday of the Year

Introduction

People generally go where they are looking! The beginning of a new year is always a good time to think about where we are going in life. One of the best ways of doing that is to think about what we are looking towards for our happiness and fulfilment. Some people look towards success in work and yet it fails so often. Others look towards possessions and there never seems enough. Others again look towards enjoyment and entertainment and often end up in loneliness and frustration.

Our Way
The Sunday Liturgy over the next few weeks calls on us to look towards Christ and in Him to find the fullness of life. This refocusing of our eyes is a constant need in the lives of Christians. If you go into a dark place it takes a long time before you can begin to see anything. Even after a time, when some things become visible you can find it difficult to move around. Your eyes play tricks on you. Then you find the light switch and everything becomes clear. That is how life is for us. Because of so much darkness of sin and hurt and lack of confidence in ourselves life can be very difficult and at times meaningless. Faith is the light switch that makes sense of it all. In the light of Christ we can see all that is most beautiful, all that is most familiar in the heart of every human person, all that is best for human life. In the light that is Christ we are set free from the darkness of sin constantly so that our own failures never need destroy us. In the light that is Christ we get healing and freedom from the effects of other people's failures on our lives and we can dare to love even our enemies. In the light that is Christ we see ourselves as we really are - wonderful, beautiful, rich people made in the image of God, loveable and loved with an infinite love of God whose only wish is that we would know how special we are.

Special Features

There are two things about the Scripture readings for these Sundays that are worth noting.

The Second Readings are all from 1 Corinthians 6-10 and 2 Corinthians 1-4. Why not read these chapters and meditate on them and catch the spirit that is there?

Most of the Gospel Readings are from Mark 1-2. As this section of the Liturgy begins, make these chapters a special part of your daily prayer so that as you prepare each week for Sunday Mass you will get drawn ever more deeply into the company of Jesus, our saviour and our brother.

SECOND SUNDAY OF THE YEAR

THEME
Answering God's call.

PRAYER FOCUS
Show us the way to peace in the world.
Question: What signs of peace do you see around us?

READINGS

1) 1 Samuel 3:3-10; 19
Speak, Lord, your servant is listening.
Question: When you pray, do you find it easy to 'listen'? What
steps could you take to help you to 'listen' more in prayer?

2) Response (to Psalm 39)
Here I am, Lord. I come to do your will.
You might pray this response as a morning offering each day.

3) 1 Corinthians 6:13-15; 17-20
Your body is the temple of the Holy Spirit.
Question: Do you believe that the Holy Spirit lives in you?
How does he affect your life?

4) John 1:35-42
'We have found the Messiah' and he took Simon to Jesus.
Question: If you met Jesus today what would you say to him?

QUESTIONS FOR ACTION

For Married Couples: Complete this sentence: I find it difficult to
listen to you when we talk about …. Why? Spend some time
listening to each other this week.

For Others: Who is it in your life that you find it hard to listen
to? Why? What change can you make this week to listen better
to that person?

THIRD SUNDAY OF THE YEAR

THEME
The ways of the Lord.

PRAYER FOCUS
That our efforts may bring humankind to unity and peace.
Question: What efforts do you make for peace in the home, and
in our country?

READINGS

1) Jonah 3:1-5; 10
Go to Nineveh and preach to them as I told you to.
Question: In what ways can you bring the message of God's love
to others?

2) Response (to Psalm 24)
Lord, make me know your ways.
Pray this response for openness
to know what God wants from you this week.

3) 1 Corinthians 7:29-31
The world as we know it is passing away.
Question: How do you feel at the death of a close friend?
Do you ever feel that things are changing very rapidly?

4) Mark 1:14-20
Follow me and I will make you into fishers of people.
Question: What do you have to do to be a 'fisher of people' in
your own circumstances?

QUESTIONS FOR ACTION

For Married Couples: In what way could you bring the gift of
your own love to another couple this week?

For Others: Have you ever considered becoming a sister, brother
or priest? Pray that many may answer his call.

FOURTH SUNDAY OF THE YEAR

THEME
The Lord, our teacher.

PRAYER FOCUS
Help us to love you with all our hearts
and to love all people as you love them.
Question: Do you think this is easy? Why?

READINGS

1) Deuteronomy 18:15-20
I will raise up a prophet from among their own.
Question: Do you know any people who are prophets in our
Church today? Do you listen to them? What is their message?

2) Response (to Psalm 94)
O that today you would listen to his voice.
Harden not your hearts.
Question: How does God speak to you?

3) 1 Corinthians 7:32-35
I would like to set you free from all worry.
Question: What worries do you have now, from which you
would like the Lord to set you tree?

4) Mark 1:21-22
He gives orders even to unclean spirits and they obey him.
Question: Do you believe this? Is it easy to pray with the
conviction that God will triumph over the evil around us?

QUESTIONS FOR ACTION

For Married Couples: What do you like best about your hus-
band/wife this week. Find a good way to let him or her know.

For Others: Is there anyone in your community who is under
stress? Find a way to listen and comfort her or him this week?

FIFTH SUNDAY OF THE YEAR

THEME
Christ who heals us.

PRAYER FOCUS
Keep us safe in your care.
Question: In what ways do you need Gods care?

READINGS

1) Job 7:1-4; 6-7
Remember that my life is but a breath.
Question: What is your reaction to this?

2) Response (to Psalm 146)
Praise the Lord who heals the broken-hearted.
Remembering someone who is broken hearted, pray this psalm
this week.

3) 1 Corinthians 9:16-19; 22-23
I made myself all things to all people.
Question: What does this mean to you? Do you think it is good
for you 'to be all things to all people'? Why?

4) Mark 1:29-39
They said to Jesus: 'Everybody is looking for you'.
Question: Do you ever feel that 'everybody is looking for you'?
When Jesus needed time for himself to reflect and pray he went
to a lonely place. Do you every take 'time away' from the hassle
of every day living? How?

QUESTIONS FOR ACTION

For Married Couples: What do you remember about your
wedding day? Take time to look at the photos and remember
together.

For Others: Think of some group that is working with youth.
How could you help them this week?

SIXTH SUNDAY OF THE YEAR

THEME
Jesus, friend of outcasts.

PRAYER FOCUS
Help us to live in your presence.
Question: How often are you aware of the presence of God in
your life? Recall one special time.

READINGS

1) Leviticus 13:1-2; 45-46
The leper must live apart; he must live outside the camp.
Question: In what areas of your life do you feel isolated and
alone? What can you do to help yourself?

2) Response (to Psalm 31)
You are my hiding place, O Lord;
you surround me with cries of deliverance.
Pray this response until you feel safe and secure in the Lord.
Question: Can you recall a time in childhood when you felt safe
and secure?

3) 1 Corinthians 10:31-11, 1
Whatever you do, do it for the glory of God.
Question: What usually motivates you to do things?

4) Mark 1:40-45
The leper said: 'If you want to, you can cure me'.
Jesus said: 'Of course I want to. Be cured'.
Question: What do you think Jesus wants to heal in your life
today? Do you want him to do this?

QUESTIONS FOR ACTION
For Married Couples: Do you pray together? If you don't already
pray together as a couple, perhaps you could try this week.
Bring to Jesus whatever area of your marriage you would like
help with.
For Others: Think of the 'lepers', outcasts in our society. Is there
any way you might help them?

SEVENTH SUNDAY OF THE YEAR

THEME
God of forgiveness.

PRAYER FOCUS
Help us to be like your Son in word and deed.
Question: How would you need to change in answer to this
prayer?

READINGS

1) Isaiah 43:18-19, 21-22, 24-25
The Lord says: No need to recall the past.
Question: In what ways are you trapped in the past?

2) Response (to Psalm 40)
Heal my soul for I have sinned against you.
Pray this response until you know this truth about yourself.

3) 2 Corinthians 1:18-22
There is no 'Yes and No' about what we say to you.
Question: In what ways do you find it difficult to commit
yourself fully to life?

4) Mark 2:1-12
Jesus said: My child, your sins are forgiven.
Question: Do you find it difficult to admit you are wrong and to
ask forgiveness?

QUESTIONS FOR ACTION
For Married Couples: Do you need to ask forgiveness fo
anything from your wife/husband? Work on this during the
coming week.
For Others: Is there anyone from whom you need forgiveness?
How could you look for it this week?

EIGHTH SUNDAY OF THE YEAR

THEME
The lover of humans.

PRAYER FOCUS
Guide the course of world events.
Question: In what ways is our world empty of God?

READINGS

1) Hosea 2:16-17, 21-22
I will betroth you to myself forever.
Question: How do you feel about this intense love of God for
you?

2) Response (to Psalm 102)
The Lord is compassion and love.
Pray this response so as to catch the wonder of it.

3) 2 Corinthians 3:1-6
You are a letter from Christ, drawn up by us.
Question: What does your life say to others about God?

4) Mark 2:18-22
Nobody puts new wine in old wineskins.
Question: What does this say to you about yourself and about
the church today?

QUESTIONS FOR ACTION

For Married Couples: In what ways has your love relationship
become dull? How could you refresh your romance this week?

For Others: Take some time this week to let nature speak to you
about the glory of God.

NINTH SUNDAY OF THE YEAR

THEME
God our strength.

PRAYER FOCUS
Keep us from danger and provide for all our needs.
Question: Why is this command important for life?

READINGS

1) Deuteronomy 5:12-15
Observe the sabbath day and keep it holy.
Question: Why is this command important for life?

2) Response (to Psalm 80)
Ring out your joy to God our strength.
Pray this until joy wells up in you.

3) 2 Corinthians 4:6-11
We are only the eartenware jars that hold this treasure.
Question: Have you ever experienced how fragile life is? When?
How?

4) Mark 2:23-3:6
The sabbath was made for people, not people for the sabbath.
Question: In what ways is your life a matter of duty, rather than
freedom?

QUESTIONS FOR ACTION
For Married Couples: In what ways could you surprise your
wife/husband in your love this week?

For Others: Do you know anyone who is burdened with
sickness? How could you reach out to that person this week?

SECTION 3

Lent

Introduction

Lent is a very special time when we are invited to travel the road to Jerusalem with Jesus. We hear his teaching calling us to repentance. We see his glory in the transfiguration. We are let into an experience of his anger and frustration with those who have turned religion into a business surrounding ritual. We are anointed with the knowledge of God's extreme love for us. And we are given the absolute assurance that Christ's death and resurrection will transform the world. It is an exciting journey, a difficult journey, an essential journey. Yet it is possible that we may not travel it because of our reluctance to leave where we are right now in our lives and in our faith.

Blocks and helps

Some people can be blocked from following Jesus fully because of the arrogance of life. They are all right the way they are and they stand in judgement on everyone else. People like this can settle for fulfilling the duties of religion but without it ever touching their hearts. Lent is a time for penance for us when we are like that, penance like fasting, like denying ourselves much of our ordinary comforts in order to realise that there is so much more to gain in life than what we have surrounded ourselves with and this is to be found in following Jesus.

Other people get blocked by their sins. They see themselves as no good, as hopeless, or they settle for a way of life that they know is unworthy of the Lord. Prayer is so vital at this time of Lent to free us from our guilt and to give us the courage to make decisions that will set us on the road with Christ. A very important part of our prayer at this time is the Sacrament of Reconciliation in which we are set free from the crippling effects of our sin.

Many other people are just too busy to travel the road with Jesus. They might do the minimum in terms of religious practice but other things tie them down. It is a full-time job making a living these days. There is so much work to be done on the house. It's so important to get the proper holidays and breaks. Where could you get the time to take Christ too seriously? During this time of Lent, alms-giving is proposed to us as very important so that, by letting go of some of our money and possessions to those in real need, we can get in touch with how well off we already are, and gain the freedom to readjust our priorities.

Conclusion

Lent can seem a burden for many of us. It is possible to use this time to discover what the real burdens are and to let Christ lift those off us that we can come to the joy of his resurrection.

FIRST SUNDAY OF LENT

THEME
The Kingdom of God is close at hand.

PRAYER FOCUS
Teach us to reflect Christ's death and resurrection in our lives.
Question: How can we reflect Christ's death and resurrection in
our lives?

READINGS

1) Genesis 9:8-15
There shall be no flood to destroy the earth again.
Question: Do you think the earth will be destroyed again? How?
Why?

2) Response (to Psalm 24)
Your ways, Lord, are faithfulness and love
for those who keep your covenant.
As you pray this remember some one who has shown God's
faithfulness to you.

3) 1 Peter 3:18-22
Christ himself died, to lead us to God.
Repeat this line slowly to yourself, using you own name Christ
himself died, to lead (your name) to God. How do you feel
about this?

4) Mark 1:12-15
Repent and believe the Good News.
Question: What one negative thought or behaviour would you
like to change this Lent to help you to fully experience God's
love?

QUESTIONS FOR ACTION
For Married Couples: What one way can you make your
wife/husband special this week? Discuss and follow through
with your plans.
For Others: Think of a relative or friend you haven't been in
touch with for some time. Make contact this week.

SECOND SUNDAY OF LENT

THEME
This is my Son, the Beloved.

PRAYER FOCUS
Enlighten us with your word that we may find
the way to your glory.
Question: Do you find that hearing and reading Scripture affects
your life? Explain?

READINGS

1) Genesis 22:1-2; 9-13; 15-18
'Here I am', Abraham replied.
Question: If God were to call you by name this week what
would your reply be? Why?

2) Response (to Psalm 115)
I will walk in the presence of the Lord in the land of the living.
Pray this response until you feel the joy and peace it brings.
Reflect back over the day and thank God for the times you
walked with the Lord.

3) Romans 8:31-34
With God on our side who can be against us?
Question: How much do I trust and treasure God as my friend
and guardian?

4) Mark 9:2-10
It is wonderful for us to be here.
Question: Have you ever felt joy like this? When?

QUESTIONS FOR ACTION
For Married Couples: Could you arrange a situation for
yourselves this week in which you can truly say, 'it is
wonderful for us to be here'. Plan this.

For Others: Recall a happy situation from your past week.
What difference did you make?

THIRD SUNDAY OF LENT

THEME
Christ, the Wisdom of God.

PRAYER FOCUS
Give us confidence in your love.
Question: How real is your confidence in God's love? Explain.

READINGS

1) Exodus 20:1-17
You shall have no Gods except me.
Question: Which 'Gods' do you think dominate our society today?

2) Response (to Psalm 18)
You, Lord, have the message of eternal life.
Question: What do you believe 'the message of eternal life' to be? Is it relevant to us today?

3) 1 Corinthians 1:22-25
God's foolishness is wiser than human wisdom.
Question: Can you recall a time when you trusted completely in God's wisdom?

4) John 2:13-25
'Stop turning my Father's house into a market', Jesus said.
Question: What is this line of Scripture saying to you today?

QUESTIONS FOR ACTION

For Married Couples: Have you a favourite place to walk? Talk about it together and if possible take a walk together and enjoy.

For Others: Try this week to thank and encourage someone you see bringing God's love to others.

FOURTH SUNDAY OF LENT

THEME
Christ, the Redeemer.

PRAYER FOCUS
Let us hasten towards Easter with the eagerness
of faith and love.
Question: What are you looking forward to most this Easter?

READINGS

1) Chronicles 36:14-16; 19-23
He wished to spare his people.
Question: Do you have patience with all the people in your life?
How do you behave when you lack patience?

2) Response (to Psalm 136)
O let my tongue cleave to my mouth if I remember you not.
Pray this response remembering God's personal love for you.

3) Ephesians 2:4-10
We are God's work of art.
Question: What do you like best about yourself? Do you believe
that you are God's work of art?

4) John 3:14-21
God sent his Son so that through him the world might be saved.
Question: God has been totally generous with us. In what ways
could you be more generous with God?

QUESTIONS FOR ACTION

For Married Couples: Say what qualities you really appreciate in
each other. Take time to appreciate the goodness in yourselves.

For Others: What do you find most difficult to share with other
people? Try at least once this week to put others before
yourself.

FIFTH SUNDAY OF LENT

THEME
The Lord's forgiveness.

PRAYER FOCUS
Father, help us to be like Christ your Son.
Question: What grace do you need to help you to 'be like Christ'
this week?

READINGS

1) Jeremiah 31:31-34
I will forgive their iniquity and never call their sin to mind.
Question: What does the sacrament of Reconciliation mean to
you?

2) Response (to Psalm 50)
A pure heart create for me, O God.
Pray this response this week asking God for help so that you
may have the strength to change in you what needs to be
changed.

3) Hebrews 5:7-9
He (Christ) became for all who obey him
the source of eternal salvation.
Question: What do you think Christ is asking of you today?

4) John 12:20-33
When I am lifted up from the earth I shall draw
all people to myself.
Question: How do you feel about Jesus dying because he loves
you? Take time to think about it this week.

QUESTIONS FOR ACTION
For Married Couples: Finish the sentence – I like it best
when you … Bring a smile to each other's face often this week.
For Others: Visit someone who has been bereaved recently.

SECTION 4

Passion Sunday –
Easter Sunday

Introduction

The central reality of our faith as Christians is that Christ has risen from the dead and that he lives among us. Holy week is the celebration of Christ's journey into this new life, a journey that we are also invited to travel knowing that he has gone before us and that he travels with us.

A difficult time

Holy Week is a difficult time for us. It is difficult because of the number of points of celebration. It is difficult because of the seriousness of the themes of the betrayal and death. And it is difficult because people are becoming more and more busy in their ordinary lives and so don't have time to enter into this occasion seriously.

It is important to make this week a special time of prayer and reflection. We do this at a community level by gathering in big numbers five times in the week. But we need to do it at a family level as well as at a personal level also. This is the week when Lenten penance should be exercised in a special way by taking this time to journey with Jesus and so catch his Spirit.

Stages of the journey

1. Palm Sunday: From being celebrated to being forgotten.
2. Holy Thursday: From giving Himself to his disciples in the Eucharist to being denied by them.
3. Good Friday: From surrendering Himself to God's will, to feeling abandoned even by God in death.
4. Holy Saturday: From complete emptiness in death to new life.
5. Easter Sunday: From the tomb to the ends of the earth.

During this Holy Week we journey through all these stages with Jesus so that he may bring us new life and hope.

PASSION SUNDAY (PALM SUNDAY)

READINGS

1) Mark 11:1-10 or John 12:12-16
2) Isaiah 50:4-7
3) Response (to Psalm 21)
My God, My God why have you forsaken me.
4) Philippians 2:6-11
5) Mark 14:1-15; 49

A THOUGHT
The crowds shouted:
(on Sunday) Hosanna! Blessings on him who comes in the name
of the Lord.
(on Friday) Crucify him! Crucify him!

QUESTIONS
Have you ever experienced the fickleness of other people?
Have you ever been guilty of it in relation to others, to Christ?

HOLY THURSDAY

READINGS

1) Exodus 12:1-8; 11-14
2) Response (to Psalm 115)
The blessing cup that we bless is a communion
with the blood of Christ.
3) 1 Corinthians 11:23-26
4) John 13:1-15

A THOUGHT
Jesus said: 'Do you understand what I have done to you'?

QUESTIONS

What is the closest you have ever felt to another person?

When have you felt closest to Christ?

GOOD FRIDAY

READINGS

1) Isaiah 52:13-53; 12
2) Response (to Psalm 30)
Father, into your hands I commend my spirit.
3) Hebrews 4:14-16; 5, 7-9
4) John 18:1-19; 42

A THOUGHT
Jesus said: 'It is accomplished'; and bowing his head
he gave up the spirit.

A QUESTION
How do you feel when you think of the crucifixion of Jesus?

HOLY SATURDAY

READINGS

1) Genesis 1:1-2, 2
2) Genesis 22:1-18
3) Exodus 14:15-15, 1
4) Isaiah 54:5-14
5) Isaiah 55:1-11
6) Baruch 3:9-15; 32-44
7) Ezechiel 36:16-17a; 18-28

NOTE
These seven readings from the Old Testament give a wonderful
knowledge of God's vision for our world and his providence in
leading us to his love.

A THOUGHT
'There is no need for alarm. He has risen, he is not here.'

A QUESTION
How does your vision for the world need to grow
so as to become more like God's vision?

EASTER SUNDAY

THEME
Joy.

PRAYER FOCUS
Let our celebration today raise us up and renew us
by the Spirit that is within us.
Question: What could prevent you from being joyful today?

READINGS

1) Acts 10:34; 37-43
Now we are those witnesses.
Question: How does your life witness to Christ?

2) Response (to Psalm 117)
This day was made by the Lord; we rejoice and are glad.
Pray this response several times, to experience the joy of it.

3) Colossians 3:1-4
Let your thoughts be on heavenly things.
Question: What does this mean to you?

4) John 20:1-9
He saw and he believed.
Question: Why do you believe?

QUESTIONS FOR ACTION

For Married Couples: What is your greatest desire for your life
together? How can you work towards that this week?

For Others: To whom could you bring some happiness this
week?

Easter 2 – Pentecost

Introduction

Over the past number of years many things have happened that could knock the heart out of us as the Church. There is a great drop in vocations to priesthood and religious life. Young people seem to reject us more and more. Scandals have hit the headlines and made many people embarrassed about being Catholics. Issues have been brought forward in the Church which make a life of faith difficult for many. It all seems endless, and we can easily end up spiritless and depressed. These weeks leading up to Pentecost open us up to another reality, that of the Risen Lord living among us and preparing us for a fresh outpouring of his Holy Spirit. With his Spirit in us nothing can ever destroy us. We become like a buoy in the stormy waters of the sea. We keep popping up again with every wave that would seem to destroy us.

Preparing for the Holy Spirit

There are many ways of thinking about the Holy Spirit. We can think of the Spirit's fruits. We can reflect on the gifts of the spirit that we share. The Liturgy during these weeks draws us into what we need to take on in order to be open to being filled again and again with the Spirit of God.

1. 'Peace be with you'. Jesus first gift of love is peace. The turmoil that we allow to take over in our lives needs to be rooted out so that this gift of Christ's peace can take over in us.
2. 'You are witnesses'. Christ gives us courage and asks us to accept it and to stand up and be counted. When we take this on we are ready for the Holy Spirit.
3. 'I am the Good Shepherd'. Jesus comforts us and carries us. It is only when we are trying to do it all ourselves that things go wrong. Our own spirit is not sufficient for the task
4. 'Bear much fruit'. Hope is a gift of the Lord that he offers us in

a special way at this time. The only way we can take this on is by casting our eyes to the horizons and opening up our own little worlds to let the huge world of possibilities enter in.

5. 'I chose you'. The intimate love of Jesus for us is the greatest knowledge of faith that we can have. The big question then becomes; where does he want us to go; how does he want us to be? And we go forward with confidence.

6. 'I share my joy with them to the full'. Our practice of faith can be so joyless. he offers us his joy and asks us to brighten up the Church for one another so that as a people of joy and fun we may be open to his Spirit.

7. 'Receive the Holy Spirit'. What a wonderful, extraordinary statement. And it is for us! The world needs us to accept this gift and let it fill that world with the glory of God.

SECOND SUNDAY OF EASTER

THEME
My Lord and my God.

PRAYER FOCUS
Renew your gifts of life within us.
Question: What are some of the blessings in your life?

READINGS

1) Acts 4:32-35
The whole group of believers was united, heart and soul.
Question: Could you say this of your family? It there something
you could do to bring unity to your family?

2) Response (to Psalm 117)
Give thanks to the Lord for he is good, for his love has no end.
As you pray this response remember some people and things in
your life that you want to give thanks for.

3) 1 John 5:1-6
Who can overcome the world?
Question: Who is Jesus for you?

4) John 20:19-31
Jesus said: Peace be with you. As the Father sent me,
so am I sending you.
Question: Where do you think Jesus is 'sending' you'? How can
you bring more peace into your life?

QUESTIONS FOR ACTION

For Married Couples: What are some of the blessings of your life
together? Share these this week.

For Others: Find out about a group working for peace. How can
you help this week?

THIRD SUNDAY OF EASTER

THEME
Our advocate with the Father.

PRAYER FOCUS
May we look forward with hope to our resurrection.
Question: In what areas of your life do you need a greater sense
of hope?

READINGS

1) Acts 3:13-15; 17-19
Now you must repent and turn to God.
Question: Do you believe that this line is being spoken to you
now? How do you feel about this?

2) Response (to Psalm 4)
Lift up the light of your face on us, O Lord.
Pray this response believing that the Lord will grant you the
favour you ask for.

3) 1 John 2:1-5
We can be sure we know God only by keeping
his commandments.
Question: What evils do you think would disappear in the world
if we kept God's commandments?

4) Luke 24:35-48
You are witnesses to all this.
Question: At what times recently have you been able to bring the
'Good News' of God's love to others by word or action?

QUESTIONS FOR ACTION

For Married Couples: What can you as a wife/husband do this
week to give the other a sense of hope in your marriage?

For Others: Think of some missionary group that brings hope
and faith to others. How could you help them this week?

FOURTH SUNDAY OF EASTER

THEME
Christ, the Good Shepherd.

PRAYER FOCUS
Give us new strength.
Question: Where do you need God's strength and courage now?

READINGS

1) Acts 4:8-12
(Jesus) is the stone rejected by you the builders.
Question: How do you see Jesus being rejected today?

2) Response (to Psalm 117)
The stone which the builders rejected
has become the corner stone.
Ask the Lord to help you to make Jesus the corner stone of your
life as you pray this response. Reflect on how this would change
your attitude to life.

3) 1 John 3:1-2
We are already the children of God.
Question: Reflect on the tender love of God for you personally.
How can you let someone else experience that this week?

4) John 10:11-18
Jesus said: I am the Good Shepherd.
Question: What does a Good Shepherd do for his sheep? Reflect
on how Jesus loves you and those around you.

QUESTIONS FOR ACTION
For Married Couples: Make a list of some of the qualities you see
in each other – share them and continue to add on fresh ones.

For Others: Do you know someone who has lost hope in any
way? What can you do to help this week?

FIFTH SUNDAY OF EASTER

THEME
Christ, the true Vine.

PRAYER FOCUS
Give us true freedom.
Question: What keeps you from being truly free in yourself and
with others?

READINGS

1) Acts 9:26-31
They were all afraid of Saul.
Question: What might keep you back from being involved in
your parish?

2) Response (to Psalm 21)
You, Lord, are my praise in the great assembly.
What are the things you want to praise God for. Keep them in
mind as you pray this response through the week.

3) 1 John 3:18-24
Our love is not to be just words or mere talk.
Question: Name one way in which you shared love recently?

4) John 15:1-8
It is to the glory of my Father that you should bear much fruit.
Question: What does this mean in your life? Is it easy to keep
Our Father's glory in focus when we act?

QUESTIONS FOR ACTION
For Married Couples: Take time to enjoy each other and show
your love by actions of deep affection and tenderness this week.
For Others: Take time to do a loving act for someone in your
family/community this week.

SIXTH SUNDAY OF EASTER

THEME
The Spirit of God's love.

PRAYER FOCUS
Help us to celebrate our joy in the resurrection of the Lord.
Question: Can you recall a time when you felt joyful recently?

READINGS

1) Acts 10:25-26; 34-35; 44-48
God does not have favourites.
Question: Do you know any people well who are not of the same
faith as yourself? Do you know anything about their beliefs?

2) Response (to Psalm 97)
The Lord has shown his salvation to the nations.
Pray this with joy and thanks.

3) 1 John 4:7-10
Let us love one another since love comes from God.
Question: Do you ever pray to God for help to change your
attitude to someone you find difficult to love?

4) John 15:9-17
You did not choose me; no, I chose you.
Question: Having put in your own name in this line and hearing
Jesus speak this to you, how for you feel about the call?

QUESTIONS FOR ACTION
For Married Couples: What do you think that Jesus has chosen
you (as a couple) to be and to do? Talk to each other about the
value of your couple love in the Church today.
For Others: Who is the most joyful priest you know? Write and
thank him for his joy in his vocation.

SEVENTH SUNDAY OF EASTER

THEME
Consecrated in the truth.

PRAYER FOCUS
That we may recognise the presence of Christ among us?
Question: When have you experienced the presence of God?

READINGS

1) Acts 1:15-17; 20-26
Lord, you can read everyone's heart.
Question: Are you comfortable with this knowledge? Explain?

2) Response (to Psalm 102)
The Lord has set his sway in heaven.
Pray this response remembering God's love for you is
unconditional.

3) 1 John 4:11-16
Anyone who lives in love, lives in God
and God lives in her/him.
Question: Whom do you know that 'lives in love'? How does
he/she show this?

4) John 17:11-19
I say these things to share my joy with them to the full.
Question: How do you feel about Jesus wanting to share his joy
with you to the full?

QUESTIONS FOR ACTION
For Married Couples: What do you do on a regular basis that
brings joy to your wife/husband? Plan a surprise for each other
this week.

For Others: Think of a group of people who pray together in the
parish. How could you be in touch with them this week?

PENTECOST SUNDAY

THEME
Receive the Holy Spirit.

PRAYER FOCUS
That the Spirit will work through our lives
to bring Christ to the world.
Question: How do you see the Spirit working in the lives of
those around you?

READINGS

1) Acts 2:1-11
They were all filled with the Holy Spirit.
Question: Recall your Confirmation Day. Which of the fruits of
the Holy Spirit, e.g. love, joy, peace, patience etc. do you think
are evident in your life?

2) Response (to Psalm 103)
Send forth your Spirit, O Lord, and renew the face of the earth.
Pray this with hope and a deep desire for it to happen.

3) 1 Corinthians 12:3-7; 12-13
The particular way in which the Spirit is given to each person
is for a good purpose.
Question: How can you best use the special gifts e.g. wisdom,
understanding, fair judgement etc. of the Holy Spirit, that you
have?

4) John 20:19-23
Receive the Holy Spirit.
Question: Do you ever pray for greater openness to the working
of the Holy Spirit in you?

QUESTIONS FOR ACTION
For Married Couples: How can you show your children how
much you love them this week? If possible recall their
Confirmation Day with them.

For Others: Think of some group that is working for young
people. How could you help them this week?

Trinity Sunday –
14th Sunday of the Year

Note:

Depending on the date of Easter in any given year, after Trinity Sunday you may have to go back to some of the later Sundays of Section 2. You then follow the sequence of Sundays through until the end of the year.

Introduction

People today are much more vocal about their lack of faith than in previous generations. Many parents particularly struggle with how to relate to their teenage son or daughter who doesn't want to go to Mass and who even at times would seem to discount the whole thing of our faith. But the fact is that faith for any of us is not easy. We can tend to make it easy by identifying it with particular actions or rituals or duties. Faith is a whole way of life that is always challenging how we have settled, and in that challenge drawing us into constant change. This is the part that is difficult.

I am with you always

During these next six weeks of the Sunday Liturgy we are put in touch with, first of all, the centre of our faith and secondly, the difficulties that are there in accepting and living that faith.

The centre of our faith is Jesus the Christ, living in us and among us today, calling us to holiness as his sisters and brothers. The way to holiness is simply to be people of the will of God. Our knowledge of the Christ present in us and with us brings us into knowing that we are always walking on sacred ground. The most sacred part of that ground is each human person we meet. Nothing should ever be more important in the practice of our faith than the dignity we give to each person, including ourselves, and the help we can give to one another to live out that dignity as the beloved of God.

Reactions

In the Sunday Liturgy there are several reactions to Jesus that we can find in ourselves today and that we need to look at and do something about. Some people were very slow to under-

stand, so Jesus patiently repeated his word to them in every way
he could think of. Others laughed at him, made fun of him for
daring to proclaim his power. There were some others, his own
relatives and neighbours, who were curious about him and pre-
tended to be interested but who rejected him because he was too
ordinary. He was just one of them and they couldn't believe.

The biggest problem of all is highlighted for us during this time
- fear. In the Scripture fear is shown as the single greatest enemy
to faith and to full life. So many times we hear that word in the
Scriptures 'Do not be afraid'. Yet fear continues to cripple us in
our letting go to Christ. Fear of what it will cost us is probably
the main one. But there is often fear of what others will say
about us; fear of failure; fear of the unknown when we realise
we have to change. During these weeks we look at those fears
and pray that the Spirit will set us, and the whole Church, free to
rejoice in the wonderful love of God.

Some features

The Second Readings are almost all from 2 Corinthians chapters
4-12 and the Gospel Readings are mainly from Mark chapters 3-
6. Read these at the beginning of the series.

TRINITY SUNDAY

THEME
Abba, Father.

PRAYER FOCUS
That our lives may bear witness to our faith.
Question: How does your life bear witness to your faith?

READINGS

1) Deuteronomy 4:32-34; 39-40
Keep his laws and commandments so that you
and your children may prosper and live long.
Question: When you think of 'Abba', 'Father', 'God' what is
your picture of Him?

2) Response (to Psalm 32)
Happy the people the Lord has chosen as his own.
Pray this response with a deep knowledge of God's love for you
personally.

3) Romans 8:14-17
The spirit himself and our spirit bear united witness
that we are children of God.
Question: What are the qualities of a good father? Can you relate
and experience these qualities in God your Father?

4) Matthew 28:16-20
Know that I am with you always.
Question: How would a real acceptance of this affect your life?

QUESTIONS FOR ACTION

For Married Couples: How can you show your children that you
love them this week.

For Others: Do something special for a child you know this
week.

TENTH SUNDAY OF THE YEAR

THEME
Mary, the model of the Church.

PRAYER FOCUS
Guide our actions in your way of peace.
Question: In what ways was Mary a woman of Peace?

READINGS

1) Genesis 3:9-15
'Where are you?', God asked.
Question: How would you answer God, in terms of your own
life now?

2) Response (to Psalm 129)
With the Lord there is mercy and fullness of redemption.
Pray this response holding up to the Lord those who need his
mercy and hope.

3) 2 Corinthians 4:13-5:1
Visible things last only for a time,
the invisible things are eternal.
Question: What are the 'invisible things that are eternal'?

4) Mark 3:20-35
Anyone who does the will of God, that person is my brother
and sister and mother.
Question: What does it mean to you to be someone's brother, sister, mother. Can you relate this to Jesus?

QUESTIONS FOR ACTION
For Married Couples: Take time for a walk together this week, to
enjoy each other and the beauty around you.

For Others: Make contact with a religious person, i.e. Brother,
Sister this week, letting them know you appreciate them.

ELEVENTH SUNDAY OF THE YEAR

THEME
Jesus, the tree of life.

PRAYER FOCUS
Help us to follow Christ and to live according to your will.
Question: What does 'God's will' mean to you?

READINGS

1) Ezekiel 17:22-24
It will sprout branches and bear fruit.
Question: Do you believe that God works in your life? How?

2) Response (to Psalm 91)
It is good to give you thanks, O Lord.
Pray this response, remembering some of the good things you
have been given by God.

3) 2 Corinthians 5:6-10
To live in the body means to be exiled from the Lord.
Question: How do you feel about your own death?

4) Mark 4:26-34
Jesus spoke the word to them so far as they were capable
of understanding it.
Question: Can you recall times when you didn't appreciate or
understand how God was working in your life?

QUESTIONS FOR ACTION

For Married Couples: Looking at your marriage can you see how
God has had a plan for you both? Discuss this with each other.

For Others: Think of some group that is working for vocations to
the religious life/priesthood. How could you encourage them
this week?

TWELFTH SUNDAY OF THE YEAR

THEME
Jesus, the Lord of the storm.

PRAYER FOCUS
Give us an unfailing respect for your name.
Question: How can you show respect for the name of Jesus?

READINGS

1) Job 38:1; 8-11
Who pent up the sea behind closed doors?
Question: What do you do when you feel hopeless?

2) Response (to Psalm 106)
Give thanks to the Lord for his love endures forever.
Pray this response until you feel a great sense of thankfulness to
God for his love for you.

3) 2 Corinthians 5:14-17
The old creation has gone, now the new one is here.
Question: What new beginnings would you like to see for
yourself in this coming week?

4) Mark 4:35-41
Jesus said: 'Why are you so frightened?'
Question: In which areas of your life are you experiencing fear?
How do you feel about Jesus saying to you, 'why are you so
frightened'?

QUESTIONS FOR ACTION

For Married Couples: What fears do you have in your married
and family life? Share them with each other this week.

For Others: Think of some groups who are helping people who
are suffering from natural disasters i.e. famine etc. Could you
help them this week?

THIRTEENTH SUNDAY OF THE YEAR

THEME
Jesus, the Lord who gives life.

PRAYER FOCUS
Keep us in the radiance of your truth.
Question: What does walking in the 'light of Christ' mean to you?

READINGS

1) Wisdom 1:13-15, 2:23-24
Death was not God's doing.
Question: Do you believe that God does not want suffering and death?

2) Response (to Psalm 29)
I will praise you, Lord, you have rescued me.
Pray this response asking him to remove all fear.

3) 2 Corinthians 8:7-9; 9:13-15
Remember how generous the Lord Jesus was.
Question: What have you in abundance, other than material things, that you can now share with your family, friends and parishioners?

4) Mark 5:21-43
They laughed at Jesus.
Question: How do you react when people ridicule you for your religious beliefs and practices?

QUESTIONS FOR ACTION

For Married Couples: How do you 'give life' to each other? Plan to make a special time for each other this week.

For Others: Think about and pray for some group that works for the promotion of life. Find a way to help them this week.

FOURTEENTH SUNDAY OF THE YEAR

THEME
Jesus despised by his own.

PRAYER FOCUS
Bring us the joy that will last forever.
Question: How do you need this prayer answered?

READINGS

1) Ezekiel 2:2-5
The spirit came into me and made me stand up.
Question: What do you need to 'stand up' for in the Church
today?

2) Response (to Psalm 122)
Our eyes are on the Lord till he shows us his mercy.
Pray this response for Northern Ireland with deep faith and
trust.

3) 2 Corinthians 12:7-10
It is when I am weak that I am strong.
Question: What do you think St Paul means by this? How do
you apply it to your own life?

4) Mark 6:1-6
Jesus was amazed at their lack of faith.
Question: Can you think of times when you had little faith in
Jesus.

QUESTIONS FOR ACTION
For Married Couples: How would you like your husband/wife to
care for you during the summer holidays? Share this and plan
this week.

For Others: Think of groups that provide holidays for children
during the summer. How can you help them at this time?

15th - 22nd Sunday of the Year

Introduction

The single greatest treasure of our Catholic faith is the Eucharist in which we are constantly invited to be totally one with Christ. He gives himself totally to us as we eat his Body and drink his Blood. The Eucharist is also a source of scandal for many and great difficulty for others. The central focus of this section of the Sunday Liturgy is the intense desire of Jesus to give us his flesh to eat and the resistance that people had to accepting Him.

Attitudes to going to Mass

Parents dread the day when their teenage son or daughter rebels and asks 'why should I go to Mass'? This is one of the best questions that could be asked, one that all of us should look at constantly. We are so conditioned by our attitudes that we can fail to ever touch into the extraordinary gift that we have. For some people Mass is an obligation on a Sunday, they go faithfully but it is an imposition, they want it over as quickly as possible. Other people see Mass as a penance, they go during the week in Lent or go to an early Mass in order to do something difficult. One of the most frequent statements that is heard about the Mass is that it is boring. How insulting we are to Jesus who has given us all of Himself and whose heart longs only to give us himself day after day, week after week. Familiarity certainly breeds contempt!

Our opportunity

These eight weeks of the Sunday Liturgy are a great opportunity to renew for ourselves a real hunger for the Eucharist. As we listen to his word during this time we can catch so much of the intimacy of his love. He recognises the loneliness and isolation of human life. He tenderly cares for each of us as if we were the only one. He knows that our human hearts can only be satisfied by being touched deeply by the quiet passion of God's love. He proclaims himself as the bread of life and goes further on promising 'the bread that I shall give is my flesh for the life of the world'. Week after week he stands among us with that wonderful invitation that has the name of each of us engraved on it. 'Take and eat, this is my Body which will be given up for you'. In that moment everything that we could want in our wildest dreams is offered to us.

Our hearts

The only problem that is presented to us during this time is that of our hearts. It is the only problem. Our hearts can be so filled with our own selfishness that there is no space for God's love. Our hearts can be so broken with life that we think there is no hope. Our hearts can be so empty because of self-doubt that we cannot hear the intense love of God. We need to open our hearts during this time. If we do, the rewards are so great as we let ourselves more into a great love affair with the Lord of the Eucharist.

FIFTEENTH SUNDAY OF THE YEAR

THEME
The Missionary Church

PRAYER FOCUS
May we reject what is contrary to the Gospel.
Question: What values do you see around today that are contrary to the Gospel?

READINGS

1) Amos 7:12-15
The Lord said 'Go Prophesy to my people'.
Question: Believing that prophet means a sign of God's love, how can you be a 'prophet' to those you meet each day?

2) Response (to Psalm 84)
Let us see, O Lord, your mercy, and give us your saving help.
In saying this response, pray for God's help in your life to bring peace to your family and the world.

3) Ephesians 1:3-14
He chose us, in Christ, to be holy.
Question: What does being holy mean to you?

4) Mark 6:7-13
So they set off to preach repentance.
Question: How can you support the Church in its Mission to bring the Good News to all people?

QUESTIONS FOR ACTION

For Married Couples: How do you bring the 'Good News' of Gods love to each other? Plan to make each other special in at least one way this week.

For Others: In what way could you help the Missionary work of the Church this week?

SIXTEENTH SUNDAY OF THE YEAR

THEME
Christ, the Good Shepherd.

PRAYER FOCUS
Make us always eager to serve you.
Question: How have you served God this week in faith, hope and love?

READINGS

1) *Jeremiah 23:1-6*
I will raise up shepherds to look after them.
Question: What qualities do you think a good shepherd has?

2) *Response (to Psalm 22)*
The Lord is my shepherd; there is nothing I shall want.
Question: Which line in this Psalm speaks clearly to you at this time? Repeat it often in prayer this week drawing on its strength.

3) *Ephesians 2:13-18*
He is the peace between us.
Question: Have you ever thought of Jesus in this way?

4) *Mark 6:30-34*
Jesus took pity on them because they were like sheep without a shepherd.
Question: How do you feel about Jesus taking pity on you? In what ways are we like sheep without a shepherd?

QUESTIONS FOR ACTION

For Married Couples: When have you last hugged each other? May this week be a time of great tenderness and peace for each other. If you have children, why not hug them and tell them how special they are to you.

For Others: Whom do you know that would appreciate some affection and affirmation this week? Take time for this.

SEVENTEENTH SUNDAY OF THE YEAR

THEME
Christ who feeds us.

PRAYER FOCUS
Help us to use wisely the blessings you have given to the world.
Question: What are the blessings that God has given us?

READINGS

1) 2 Kings 4:42-44
The Lord says: 'they will eat and have some left over'.
Question: How do you respond to the terrible hunger that many
people experience today?

2) Response (to Psalm 144)
You open wide your hand, O Lord, and grant our desires.
Pray this response in thanksgiving for all the blessings you have
received.

3) Ephesians 4:1-6
I implore you to live a life worthy of your vocation.
Question: In everyday living what does this mean to you?

4) John 6:1-15
Jesus said: 'where can we buy some food
for these people to eat?'
Question: In relation to the 'Third World' how would you
personally respond to this question of Jesus?

QUESTIONS FOR ACTION

For Married Couples: Reflect on what you hunger for in your
relationship, e.g. more time together, more conversation.
Talk about this and listen to each other this week.

For Others: Find some way this week of helping a group who
work to feed the starving.

EIGHTEENTH SUNDAY OF THE YEAR

THEME
Bread from heaven.

PRAYER FOCUS
Forgive our sins and restore us to life.
Question: How will having this prayer answered affect your
life?

READINGS

1) Exodus 16:2-4, 12-15
The whole community began to complain
against Moses and Aaron.
Question: Do you ever complain about how you see God
working in the world? Do you ever complain to God in prayer?

2) Response (to Psalm 77)
The Lord gave them bread from heaven.
Pray this response thinking of God's love for us shown in the
Eucharist.

3) Ephesians 4:17; 20-24
Your mind must be renewed by a spiritual revolution.
Question: In what ways do you see your life drifting in an
aimless way? In what small way might you change this?

4) John 6:24-35
Do not work for food that cannot last but work for food that
endures to eternal life.
Question: How important is the Eucharist in your life?

QUESTIONS FOR ACTION
For Married Couples: Recall three joyful times you had together.
Make time for one more this week.

For Others: Make two visits this week, one to a church and one
to a person who would be glad of a visit from you.

NINETEENTH SUNDAY OF THE YEAR

THEME
I am the bread of life.

PRAYER FOCUS
Increase your spirit within us.
Question: What does this mean for your life?

READINGS

1) 1 Kings 19:4-8
'Get up and eat, or the journey will be too long for you'.
Question: How does the reception of Holy Communion help
you on your journey of life?

2) Response (to Psalm 33)
Taste and see that the Lord is good.
Question: Pray this response until you feel the joy and peace that
Jesus brings.

3) Ephesians 4:30-5:2
Never have grudges against others, or lose your temper.
Question: What helps you to let go of grudges or to be at peace
with others?

4) John 6:41-51
Jesus said: 'I am the bread of life. The bread that I shall give is
my flesh for the life of the world'.
Question: Reflect on Jesus saying this to you personally. How do
you feel about this?

QUESTIONS FOR ACTION

For Married Couples: When did you last have a romantic
evening? Recall it. Plan another one for this week.

For Others: Is there someone for whom you hold a grudge, or
with whom you are not at peace? Do something to rectify that,
this week.

TWENTIETH SUNDAY OF THE YEAR

THEME
Anyone who eats this bread will live forever.

PRAYER FOCUS
May we love you in all things and above all things.
Question: How do you think that loving God this way would
change our lives?

READINGS

1) Proverbs 9:1-6
Leave your folly and you will live.
Question: Are there any ways in which you spend timefoolishly?

2) Response (to Psalm 33)
Taste and see that the Lord is good.
Pray this response that your meeting with Jesus in the Eucharist
will be a more meaningful experience this week.

3) Ephesians 5:15-20
Be careful about the sort of lives you lead.
Question: Reflect back over yesterday from the moment you got
up. How was that day for you? Don't be harsh on yourself.
Thank Jesus for walking with you.

4) John 6:51-58
Jesus said: 'Whoever eats me will draw life from me.'
Question: How do you feel about Jesus saying this to you?

QUESTIONS FOR ACTION
For Married Couples: In what ways will you bring the love of
Jesus to each other this week? Be specific.

For Others: How do you spend your time? Is there any change
you could make this week so as to give some time to another
person?

TWENTY-FIRST SUNDAY OF THE YEAR

THEME
You are the Holy One of God.

PRAYER FOCUS
Make us one in mind and heart.
Question: What makes it difficult/easy for you to follow Christ
in the way he wants?

READINGS

1) Joshua 24:1-2, 15-18
'If you will not serve the Lord, choose today whom you wish
to serve' Joshua said to all the people.
Question: What does 'Serving the Lord' mean to you? What
other choices do you see around for us today?

2) Response (to Psalm 33)
Taste and see that the Lord is good.
Pray this response often remembering that you live in Jesus and
he lives in you.

3) Ephesians 5:21-32
Give way to one another in obedience to Christ.
Question: How do you feel about Saint Paul saying this to you
today?

4) John 6:60-69
Simon Peter said: 'Lord, to whom shall we go? You have the
message of eternal life, and we believe.'
Question: When do you 'go' to Jesus? What causes you to stop
turning to him?

QUESTIONS FOR ACTION
For Married Couples: What gift could you give to your wife/
husband this week?

For Others: Pray this week for all couples that they may love
each other tenderly, gently. Perhaps you could enable a couple
to take time out for themselves.

TWENTY-SECOND SUNDAY OF THE YEAR

THEME
The Commandments of Life.

PRAYER FOCUS
Protect the good you have given us.
Question: How good has God been to you?

READINGS

1) Deuteronomy 4:1-2, 6-8
What great nation is there that has its gods so near as the Lord
our God is to us whenever we call to him?
Question: When did you last feel God's presence with you?

2) Response (to Psalm 14)
Lord, who shall be admitted to your tent?
Pray this response thinking about the joy of being with Jesus in
heaven forever.

3) James 1:17-18; 21-22; 27
Accept and submit to the word that has been planted in you
and can save your souls.
Question: Which line in this Scripture Passage speaks most
clearly to you? Take time to reflect on the word that 'has been
planted in you'.

4) Mark 7:1-8; 14-15; 21-23
These people honours me only with lip-service while their
hearts are far from me.
Question: In our country today where do you find people
paying only lip service to Christ's teaching?

QUESTIONS FOR ACTION
For Married Couples: Recall some good times from your
holidays. Plan to continue to create romance for each other as
you move into the Autumn term. How can you do this?
For Others: Take time out for yourself this week to be at peace –
a walk, time on your own etc.

23rd - 28th Sunday of the Year

Introduction

Someone has said that it's not so much that Christianity has failed as that it was never tried. There's a lot of truth in that statement. We are forever reducing Christianity to religious rituals that we can fulfil with relative ease and to laws that we can try to keep, with perhaps greater difficulty. But Christianity is a whole way of life of following Jesus, being formed by his word, trusting in faith that the way he points out will indeed lead to full life. This section of the Sunday Liturgy opens up some of the primary implications of that way.

Values of life

Our values are generally seen in what we are aiming for in life. The values of Christ are often different from the ones we settle for because he gives us something different to aim for. His desire for all of us is full life.

1. Self-fulfilment is the aim of many people today and it's a good aim to have. But when it becomes the object of life it becomes very selfish. Jesus gives us as the aim of life to fulfil one another. Obviously that cannot be done if it is imposed on us or unless we have inner freedom.

2. Independence is what most people are looking for in life, both as individuals and as communities. Again this is a good longing but it is not the ultimate. Jesus gives us, as his way, a call to love and to live a life of interdependence and of unity. We cannot live like that unless we have moved through to the point of independence. Love has to be a free surrender to one another.

3. Privacy is a very important value of our world and it is a real good that is denied so many people. When it becomes the aim of life it deteriorates into an imprisonment where there is so much loneliness. Sharing what we have is the way of the Lord. It is only in that way that we stay free.

4. Equality is being sought today as never before, especially the equality of women and men. This is a very good, essential development in human history. But even that is not the greatest objective in the way of Christ. Giving way to one another is his way. Making the other person number one is how he wants us to be. This is especially true in marriage. But it runs through all our relationships.

5. To be yourself is what our society holds up as the aim of life. Jesus teaches us his way that of forgetting yourself, emptying yourself. But of course you can only do that when you know yourself and can accept yourself as good.

Some features

The Gospel Readings during this time are all from Mark chapters 7-10. Read these chapters and catch the excitement of this journey with Christ.

The Second Readings are mainly from James chapters 2-5. It is a good time to read this whole letter and enter into the on-going struggle between faith and good works.

TWENTY-THIRD SUNDAY OF THE YEAR

THEME
The Lord who does all things well.

PRAYER FOCUS
Give us true freedom.
Question: What does 'true freedom' mean to you?

READINGS

1) Isaiah 35:4-7
Courage, do not be afraid.
Question: In what areas of your life do you need courage and
lack of fear?

2) Response (to Psalm 145)
My soul, give praise to the Lord.
Pray this response thinking of some of the things you want to
thank and praise God for this week.

3) James 2:1-5
Do not try to combine faith in Jesus with the making
of distinctions between classes of people.
Question: What groups of people do you find difficult to accept?
How do you think Jesus would respond to these people?

4) Mark 7:31-37
He makes the deaf hear and the dumb speak.
Question: Whom do you find difficult to communicate with?

QUESTIONS FOR ACTION
For Married Couples: In what ways could you be more free with
each other? Share this.

For Others: Pray for those in prison. Perhaps you could write a
letter to someone in prison or visit a lonely housebound person.

TWENTY-FOURTH SUNDAY OF THE YEAR

THEME
Christ, the Son of Man.

PRAYER FOCUS
May we serve you with all our hearts.
Question: How can you serve God in others this coming week?

READINGS

1) Isaiah 50:5-9
I offered my back to those who struck me.
Question: How do I react when I feel hurt and misunderstood?

2) Response (to Psalm 114)
I will walk in the presence of the Lord, in the land of the living.
Pray this response daily and reflect at the end of the day on the
times you tried to walk in his presence.

3) James 2:14-18
If good works do not go with faith, it is quite dead.
Question: What does 'good works' mean to you in your every
day life? How does your faith affect your good works?

4) Mark 8:27-35
If anyone wants to be a follower of mine, let him/her renounce
herself/himself, take up his/her cross and follow me.
Question: What crosses have you borne this week? How did you
cope with them? Did you ask Jesus for help?

QUESTIONS FOR ACTION

For Married Couples: Share with each other what dreams you
have for your future together.

For Others: Pray for someone whom you know to be suffering at
this time. Visit him/her if possible this week.

TWENTY-FIFTH SUNDAY OF THE YEAR

THEME
Christ, the Son of God.

PRAYER FOCUS
May we love one another.
Question: What does 'love one another' mean in your life right now?

READINGS

1) Wisdom 12:17-20
The godless say: 'Let us lie in wait for the virtuous person ...'.
Question: In which ways can you sense the power of evil in the world today?

2) Response (to Psalm 53)
The Lord upholds my life.
Pray this response asking the Lord to keep you safe from all evil.

3) James 3:16-43
Wherever you find jealousy and ambition you find disharmony.
Question: What can you do this week to bring peace to those around you?

4) Mark 9:30-37
If anyone wants to be first, he/she must make him/herself least of all and servant of all.
Question: What qualities do little children have that we might imitate?

QUESTIONS FOR ACTION

For Married Couples: Recall some memories of childhood for each other. Do something this week you enjoyed doing as a child, e.g. a walk on the beach to gather shells.

For Others: Take time to wonder at the beauty of a baby or small child. Could you baby-sit for someone this week?

TWENTY-SIXTH SUNDAY OF THE YEAR

THEME
God's Spirit in the world.

PRAYER FOCUS
Continue to fill us with your gifts of love.
Question: Can you remember experiencing the gifts of God's
love during last week?

READINGS

1) Numbers 11:25-29
When the spirit came on them they prophesied.
Question: How does the Spirit work in your life?

2) Response (to Psalm 18)
The precepts of the Lord gladden the heart.
Pray this response with thanksgiving for the times you have fol-
lowed his ways.

3) James 5:1-6
An answer for the rich: your wealth is all rotting.
Question: What is important in your life?

4) Mark 9:38-43; 45; 47-48
Anyone who is not against us is for us.
Question: Is it easy to be a disciple of Jesus at this time? What
helps are available to you?

QUESTIONS FOR ACTION
For Married Couples: Think of ways to show your husband/wife
that you are not taking him/her for granted.
For Others: What are some of your personal qualities? How can
you use them for others this week?

TWENTY-SEVENTH SUNDAY OF THE YEAR

THEME
The family of God

PRAYER FOCUS
Forgive our failings.
Question: Do you believe that God loves you as you are? Do you
accept your own failings?

READINGS

1) Genesis 2:18-24
This is why a man leaves his father and mother
and joins himself to his wife and they become one body.
Question: How important do you see marriage to be, in the
Church today?

2) Response (to Psalm 127)
May the Lord bless us all the days of our life.
Pray this response often with certain knowledge that
he will answer your prayer.

3) Hebrews 2:9-11
He openly calls them brothers and sisters.
Question: How do you feel about Jesus calling you
'brother' 'sister'?

4) Mark 10:2-16
They are no longer two, therefore, but one body.
Question: Is it enough for a married couple to be one in body?
What else is needed?

QUESTIONS FOR ACTION
For Married Couples: How can you grow in sexual love this
week?

For Others: Think of some group who is working for the support
of marriage. How could you support them this week?

TWENTY-EIGHTH SUNDAY OF THE YEAR

THEME
Christian values.

PRAYER FOCUS
Make us eager to do good for others.
Question: How eager are you to love yourself as well as loving others.

READINGS

1) Wisdom 7:7-11
I entreated, and the spirit of wisdom came to me.
Question: In what areas of your life do you need to pray for the Spirit of Wisdom?

2) Response (to Psalm 89)
Fill us with your love that we may rejoice.
Pray this response thinking of ways to rejoice in God's love this coming week.

3) Hebrews 4:12-13
The word of God is something alive and active.
Question: How do you feel about this? Have you experienced God's word speaking to you in Scripture?

4) Mark 10:17-30
'Good Master, what must I do to inherit eternal life?'
Question: What reply does Jesus make to you personally?

QUESTIONS FOR ACTION
For Married Couples: Recall your courting days and things you did to make each other special.
For Others: Think of someone who touched your life recently – find a way of saying thanks this week.

29th Sunday -
Christ the King

Introduction

So many people live in very small worlds, sometimes of their own making, at other times forced onto them. One of the signs of living in a small world is where mole-hills are made into mountains. No one can live without mountains. In a small world mole-hills suffice. Jesus introduces us into a very big world as his followers. The ends of the earth are our horizons. Eternal life is our hope.

What is eternal life?

We tend to think of eternal life only as what will happen after death. No one is in any hurry to get to it. As the song puts it: 'Everybody wants to go to heaven but nobody wants to die'. Death is a part of life that scares us all and yet it is inevitable. It looks like the end. Jesus gives us the assurance that it is only the beginning. It is like putting out the candle because the lights have been switched on. That knowledge of faith doesn't make death attractive, but it does put it into context. We are not just destined for now but forever.

Eternal life and happiness forever is going to take many people by surprise. Can you imagine having to be happy all the time? It'll be torture for those who have practised being miserable! Imagine being with people for all eternity and not a fault to be found anywhere. It'll be hell for those of us whose main occupation is talking about what's wrong with the world and with those around us.

Begin now

Eternal life has to be practised for and now is the time to begin. The Liturgy of these Sundays highlights some of the ways of doing that and of actually living eternal life now.

The first way is to forget our own self-importance and enjoy all that life has to offer. We get so caught up in ourselves that life can pass us by. The happiest person is the one who can be glad of who they are now and rejoice in all the wonderful, simple things of life that even a servant has.

The second thing is to recognise our own short-sightedness and often blindness. We can think that the only reality is what we can see ourselves. Our own opinions become the truth. We are very limited by ourselves. It is only through the power of God that we expand.

Thirdly we need to set our sights on what is most important in life. Jesus is very clear on what that is: to love God with our whole heart, our whole soul, our whole mind, our whole strength and to love our neighbour as ourselves. When our sights are fixed there we gain true freedom.

And then Jesus teaches us generosity with one another as vital for the journey. We get possessed by our possessions. We need to be able to give them away because we cannot bring them with us.

All of this is in the setting of our knowledge that Jesus is with us. He is our King. He is our Lord. He is our Saviour and he walks with us. Nothing can ever destroy us.

Some Features

The Gospel Readings for these Sundays are almost all from Mark chapters 10-13. Read these chapters many times during these weeks. You will find great inspiration there.

The Second Readings are taken from Hebrews chapters 4-10. This whole letter should be read so as to catch the spirit of adventure there is in being the Church.

TWENTY-NINTH SUNDAY OF THE YEAR

THEME
Christian Ambition.

PRAYER FOCUS
Give us strength and joy in serving you.
Question: What difference would 'strength' and 'joy' make in
your life now?

READINGS

1) Isaiah 53:10-11
By his suffering shall my servant justify many.
Question: What does this tell you of the great love and ambition
that Our Father has for you personally?

2) Response (to Psalm 32)
May your love be upon us, O Lord,
as we place all our hope in you.
Pray this response often during the week
in complete trust and hope.

3) Hebrews 4:14-16
We must never let go of the faith we have professed.
Question: What works against us holding on to our faith
in society today?

4) Mark 10:35-45
Anyone who wants to be great among you
must be your servant.
Question: What is your ambition for the next year?
How does God fit into this?

QUESTIONS FOR ACTION

For Married Couples: What do you want for yourselves as a
couple this coming week? Share this with each other.

For Others: What is your ambition for the Church in your parish
at this time and what can you do to make this come to fruition?

THIRTIETH SUNDAY OF THE YEAR

THEME
Christian hope.

PRAYER FOCUS
Strengthen our faith, hope and love.
Question: How would you like this prayer answered?

READINGS

1) Jeremiah 31:7-9
The Lord has saved his people.
Question: What is your idea of God the Father?

2) Response (to Psalm 125)
What marvels the Lord worked for us. Indeed we were glad.
Pray this response remembering times when you experienced
Joy and said 'thanks be to God'.

3) Hebrews 5:1-6
He can sympathise with those who are ignorant or uncertain.
Question: What is our attitude to those who are 'ignorant' or
'uncertain' in our society?

4) Mark 10:46-52
Jesus asked: 'What do you want me to do for you?'
Question: Allow Jesus to ask you this question today. What is
your reply?

QUESTIONS FOR ACTION

For Married Couples: What are the signs of hope in your
marriage? How can you bring hope to each other this week?

For Others: Do you know someone who has lost hope at this
time? Can you bring some hope to them this week?

THIRTY-FIRST SUNDAY OF THE YEAR

THEME
Christian faith.

PRAYER FOCUS
May we live the faith we profess.
Question: What does this prayer mean to you?

READINGS

1) Deuteronomy 6:2-6
You shall love the Lord, your God, with all your heart.
Question: In your daily life how can you do this?

2) Response (to Psalm 17)
I love you, Lord, my strength.
Pray this very slowly until you absorb and feel the words take
root.

3) Hebrews 7:23-28
His power to save is utterly certain.
Question: Do you believe that Jesus has saved you? How does
this affect your life?

4) Mark 12:28-34
'Which is the first of all the commandments?'
Question: What keeps you from fully living out this first
commandment?

QUESTIONS FOR ACTION

For Married Couples: Do you use the gift of touch in your general
communication? Plan to use it with each other this coming
week.

For Others: Think of a group that is working for the renewal of
the Church. How could you support them this week?

THIRTY-SECOND SUNDAY OF THE YEAR

THEME
Christian trust.

PRAYER FOCUS
Give us freedom of spirit and health in mind and body.
Question: In what ways do you want this prayer answered?

READINGS

1) 1 Kings 17:10-16
Do not be afraid.
Question: In what areas of your life do you need to listen to Our
Father saying to you 'Do not be afraid'.

2) Response (to Psalm 145)
My soul, give praise to the Lord.
Pray this response constantly in thanksgiving for some special
grace or happening in your life.

3) Hebrews 9:24-28
Christ came 'that he might appear in the actual presence
of God on our behalf'.
Question: How do you feel about Jesus going to God on your
behalf?

4) Mark 12:38-44
'From the little she had she has put in everything'.
Question: What keeps you from giving all to others in terms of
yourself, time, money etc?

QUESTIONS FOR ACTION
For Married Couples: Make a list of things you want to thank
each other for. Share this list.

For Others: Think of some group that is working for adult
education in the faith. How could you support and encourage
them this week?

THIRTY-THIRD SUNDAY OF THE YEAR

THEME
Eternal life, the Christian vision.

PRAYER FOCUS
Keep us faithful in serving you.
Question: What does this prayer mean to you?

READINGS

1) Daniel 12:1-3
There is going to be a time of great distress.
Question: Is there great distress around us today? What signs of
hope do you see?

2) Response (to Psalm 15)
Preserve me, God, I take refuge in you.
Pray this response often as a prayer for peace in our country
and world.

3) Hebrews 10:11-14; 18
Christ has offered one single sacrifice for sins.
Question: How do you feel about this? What is your vision of
heaven?

4) Mark 13:24-32
Know he is near, at the very gate.
Question: What does this mean for you?

QUESTIONS FOR ACTION

For Married Couples: Do you know a widow or widower living
alone? Could you call on them or bring him or her to your home
for coffee etc?

For Others: Do you know someone who has been bereaved
recently? What can you do to help?

LAST SUNDAY OF THE YEAR

THEME
Christ the King.

PRAYER FOCUS
That all men and women will acclaim Jesus as Lord.
Question: What difference would there be in our world if all
people acclaimed Jesus as Lord?

READINGS

1) Daniel 7:13-14
His empire will never be destroyed.
Question: What is your vision of Christ as King?

2) Response (to Psalm 92)
The Lord is King, with majesty enrobed.
Pray this response acknowledging Christ as King of your life.

3) Apocalypse 1:5-8
He loves us and has washed away our sins with his blood
Question: Can you take time to reflect on the tremendous love of
Jesus for us and for you personally. How do you feel about it?

4) John 18:33-37
All who are on the side of truth listen to my voice.
Question: In what ways does Jesus speak to us today.

QUESTIONS FOR ACTION

For Married Couples: Looking back over the past year take time
to ask forgiveness for patterns of behaviour that might have
caused loneliness to each other. Plan to bring hope to each other
this week.

For Others: Think of some group that is working for the homeless and destitute. How can you help this group this week?

Year C

SECTION 1

Advent 1 - The Baptism of the Lord

Introduction

'Watch yourselves! Stay awake!'

As we begin another year of the Church's journey of faith, it is important to listen to and to take heed of these words of Jesus. They are not so much words of condemnation as words of invitation. Jesus' great desire is that we, both personally and as a community, would have life and have it to the full. The great enemy of this desire is the way in which we can drift in our own lives and in our relationships with one another.

Advent

These four weeks are given to us to come alive to the wonderful gifts that God has given us. In practice it is often a time when people are looking at all the things they *don't* have. The advertisers are in full flight. The message is loud and clear that if you don't get all these latest products you will be miserable. And we believe it! We already have all that it takes to be happy. We have life, but we take it for granted. We have health, but we talk about our pains. We have people who love us, but we highlight how they hurt us. We have so much to live for, but we live in the past. Advent is a time for looking ahead and catching again the excitement of life.

Christmas

People keep saying that Christmas is for children. It has become that, but it shouldn't be. Christmas is about a child who calls us to adult, mature responses to God and his love for us. It is a time of laziness for many adults. This is only symptomatic of the spiritual laziness that can be in our lives the whole year round. Christmas is a call to stir ourselves out of this spiritual stupor and let our minds and hearts be fired up by this most extraordinary event. A child is born for us, a saviour is given to us. God is very close to us and wants passionately to lift us into life.

The Baptism of the Lord

So many of us live in a very small world of our own concerns. The big world beyond us can be of little concern to us in our daily lives. We hardly ever notice the beauty of creation. We are seldom pained by the hardships of those who suffer hunger or who are caught up in violence and destruction. This whole section of the liturgical year has been leading us to this point of the Baptism and mission of Jesus our Lord. The child born for us at Bethlehem is sent to turn the world upside down. He baptises us with the Holy Spirit and with fire for that same mission. The characteristic of the church has to be a people on fire with love for God and for every human person; an enthusiastic people; a hope-filled people; a humble people. How dare we attempt to reduce the whole thing again to religious practices carried out reluctantly.

Some Features

Joy is the grace that runs through many of the prayers of the Sundays in this section. Why not make that our quest during this time? The gospel readings are all from Luke, 1-3 and 24. It would be helpful to read these in full so that, week by week, we can be drawn fully into the Lord's journey among us.

FIRST SUNDAY OF ADVENT

THEME
Our Liberation from fear

PRAYER FOCUS
Increase our strength of will for doing good.
Question: What are the things that make it difficult for you to
keep going. Pray about these.

READINGS

1) Jeremiah 33:14-16
Israel shall dwell in confidence.
Question: What is needed to bring greater confidence to your
faith and that of your community.

2) Response (to Psalm 24)
To you, O Lord I lift up my soul.
Pray this response until you can know the presence of the Lord.

3) 1 Thessalonians 3:12-4:2
Love one another and the whole human race as we love you.
Question: What limits do you set to love?

4) Luke 21:25-28; 34-36
Hold your heads high, because your liberation is close at hand.
Question: Do you get despondent because of the problems of the
world? How do you handle this?

QUESTIONS FOR ACTION

For Married Couples: In what ways would you like to have
greater freedom in your relationship with your wife/husband?
(Share these this week.)

For Others: Do you know anyone who is 'imprisoned' in any
way? (Contact them this week.)

SECOND SUNDAY OF ADVENT

THEME
The joy of salvation.

PRAYER FOCUS
Remove what hinders us from receiving Christ with joy.
Question: What does this mean to you in your own life?

READINGS

1) Baruch 5:1-9
Jerusalem, Take off your dress of sorrow and distress.
Question: How could you be more cheerful as a family
and community?

2) Response (to Psalm 125)
What marvels the Lord worked for us!
Indeed we are glad.
Pray this response while counting your blessings.

3) Philippians 1:3-6; 8-11
So that you can always recognise what is best.
Question: Do you seek out what is best for those you love or just
settle for whatever happens?

4) Luke 3:1-6
All mankind shall see the salvation of God.
Question: How enthusiastic are you that the world would know
the wonder of Christ?

QUESTIONS FOR ACTION
For Married Couples: How could you help to keep a smile on the
face of your wife/husband this week?

For Others: What do you need to do so that you can be
particularly cheerful this week?

THIRD SUNDAY OF ADVENT

THEME
A day of festival

PRAYER FOCUS
May we experience the joy of salvation
Question: What could prevent you from joy today?

READINGS

1) Zephaniah 3:14-18
Rejoice, exult with all your heart.
Question: How can you bring a sense of this joy and happiness
to your home and community?

2) Response (to Isaiah 12:2-6)
Sing and shout for joy for great in your midst
is the holy one of Israel.
Pray this until you are free of any reluctance to being happy.

3) Philippians 4:4-7
I want you to be happy, always happy in the Lord.
Question: Is that your ambition for yourself and your loved
ones?

4) Luke 3:10-18
What about us? What must we do?
Question: What do you need to do so that you can be more for
God and for others?

QUESTIONS FOR ACTION

For Married Couples: How can you be really romantic for your
wife/husband this week?

For Others: To whom could you bring a sense of joy and well-
being this week?

FOURTH SUNDAY OF ADVENT

THEME
Mary's child – The Prince of Peace

PRAYER FOCUS
Fill our hearts with your love.
Question: What is your heart like right now?

READINGS

1) Micah 5:1-4
He himself will be peace.
Question: With so much conflict around us, what does that
prophesy mean to you?

2) Response (to Psalm 79)
God of hosts bring us back, let your face shine on us
and we shall be saved.
Pray this until you know how you and we need God.

3) Hebrews 10:5-10
'God, here I am! I am coming to obey your will'.
Question: What do you think 'God's will' means?

4) Luke 1:39-44
Blessed is she who believed that the promise made her
by the Lord would be fulfilled.
Question: How important is Mary in your life? Why?

QUESTION FOR ACTION

For Married Couples: In what ways is there any distance between
you and your wife/husband just now? What will you do about
it this week?

For Others: How will you create a great sense of peace for those
closest to you this week?

CHRISTMAS DAY

THEME
A Saviour is born for us.

PRAYER FOCUS
Bring us to eternal joy in the kingdom of heaven.
Question: Is there anything disturbing you at this time?

READINGS

1) Isaiah 9:2-7
Wide is his dominion in a peace that has no end.
Question: How can this prophesy be fulfilled in our world?

2)Response (to Psalm 95)
To-day a Saviour has been born for us; he is Christ the Lord.
Pray this until you are filled with the wonder of it.

3) Titus 2:11-14
That we 'would have no ambition except to do good.'
Question: What are the ambitions of your life?

4) Luke 2:1-14
'Do not be afraid, listen, I bring you news of great joy,
a joy to be shared by the whole people.'
Question: What will prevent many people from true joy today?

QUESTIONS FOR ACTION

For Married Couples: How can you make this Christmas very
special for your wife/husband?

For Others: Is there someone you could contact today by a visit
or a phone call who would really appreciate your call?

HOLY FAMILY

THEME
Jesus, Mary and Joseph

PRAYER FOCUS
Help us to be united in respect and love.
Question: What do you need for this to grow in your family?

READINGS

1) *Ecclesiasticus 3:2-6; 12-14*
Long life comes to him who honours his father, he who sets
his mother at ease is showing obedience to the Lord.
Question: How can you develop your relationship with or your
memories of your parents?

2) *Response (to Psalm 127)*
O Blessed are those who fear the Lord and walk in his ways.
Pray this response until you can feel the strength of it.

3) *Colossians 3:12-21*
Forgive each other as soon as a quarrel begins.
Question: Is there anyone in your family
whom you need to forgive?

4) *Luke 2:41-52*
His mother stored up all these things in her heart.
Question: What are some of your nicest memories of
your parents as you grew up?

QUESTIONS FOR ACTION

For Married Couples: What are some of the nicest things you
know about the parents of your wife/husband? Share these
with each other and if possible with them.

For Others: How could you contact each member of your family
this week?

SECOND SUNDAY AFTER CHRISTMAS

THEME
Christ, the wisdom of God.

PRAYER FOCUS
Fill the world with your splendour
and show the nations the light of your truth.
Question: How eager are you for this prayer to be answered?

READINGS

1) Sirach 24:1-4, 12-16
I have taken root in a privileged people.
Question: Do you recognise the privilege it is to belong to the
Church? Why/Why not?

2) Response (to Psalm 147)
The word was made flesh and lived among us.
Pray this response until you feel the excitement of it.

3) Ephesians 1:3-6, 15-18
May he enlighten the eyes of your mind
so that you can see what hope his call holds for you.
Question: When have you been most hopeful about life?

4) John 1:1-18
He was in the world and the world did not know him.
Question: Why do people find it difficult to accept Christ?

QUESTIONS FOR ACTION
For Married Couples: What were the beginnings of your love for
each other? Take time to share on this during the week.

For Others: Do you know anyone for whom Christmas has been
difficult? How could you reach out to them this week?

BAPTISM OF THE LORD

THEME
'You are my son, the beloved.'

PRAYER FOCUS
Keep us faithful to our calling.
Question: What do you see as your calling?

READINGS

1) Isaiah 42:1-4; 6-7
I have endowed him with my spirit that he may bring true justice to the nations.
Question: What are the sources of injustice in our world?

2) Response (to Psalm 28)
The Lord will bless his people with peace.
Pray this until you become sure of it.

3) Acts 10:34-38
Jesus Christ is Lord of all people.
Question: Why do so many seem to reject him?

4) Luke 3:15-16; 21-22
He will baptise you with the Holy Spirit and fire
Question: What limits do you set on your life of faith?

QUESTIONS FOR ACTION

For Married Couples: What three things would you like to see happen in your marriage relationship this year? Tell your wife/husband this week.

For Others: What could your read this week that would be helpful for your faith.

2nd - 8th Sunday
of the Year

Introduction

'Fill the jars with water'

This command, 'Fill the jars with water' is given to us on the first Sunday of this section. It was first given to the servants at the wedding feast of Cana. It continues to be given to every generation of Christ's followers. But what does it mean for us? I suggest that there are six main priorities for us today to work at so that the Church may be a source of life and hope to our world.

1. Community

Our major response to Christ as his followers is to build community in every way that is possible. This is in response to his deepest longing, expressed in his passionate prayer: 'Father, may they be one.' It is also the deepest experience of the Church that we are saved and sent as a community, as a people. And the world in which we live badly needs community, even as it moves further away from it. But this needs to be a *priority*, and not just a gesture.

2. Ecumenism

This is not optional for Catholics. It is an integral part of the practice of our faith. And yet, in reality, ecumenism, the unity of all Christ's followers, is not taken seriously. We cannot move forward unless and in so far as we are working at this as a priority of faith.

3. Marriage and family life

With so much talk about marriage breakdown, we can easily lose confidence in this most intimate way of human living. We do so at our peril. Marriage is pivotal to how we know God and live with and in Christ. The home is called the Domestic Church, the place where the Church is at its best and worst. Supporting and encouraging marriage and family life should be a characteristic of our life of faith, and not just when things go wrong, but especially so that things can go right. But we can easily pay lip-service to it.

4. Justice and Peace

Jesus's mission was to bring good news to the poor and freedom to those in captivity of any kind. The social teaching of the Church is outstanding, and yet it has very little impact on the lives of many Catholics. We have to be seen in the front lines of the fight to bring justice and freedom and dignity to every human person. Otherwise we are not believable as Christ's followers.

5. Empowerment of the laity

We are still a very clerical Church. The priest has a very important place in the Church but so do the laity. The only trouble is that we don't know what that place of the laity is because we have got so used to being Church in a particular way. The laity are not just to help the priest in his duties, especially when there is a shortage of priests. The laity need to be led and set free to take on full responsibility for their faith, their parish, their world. Otherwise we remain apart from real life.

6. Young people

We need to win our young people, otherwise we grow old and become irrelevant. Young people keep the Church on her toes by the questions they ask, the opinions they express, the life-style they live. Having young people among us in any real sense means that we will always have to keep changing, not the essentials, obviously, but the trappings that can so easily become essentials. A Church that is not changing constantly has very little to say to our world.

These are some of the main priorities of our Church today. The great enemy of them is spoken about on the Eighth Sunday, namely our quarrels with one another and how we take revenge. During these Sundays we have a chance to set our sights again and clear the ground so that we can move forward freely together.

Some Features

The Second Readings for these Sundays are all taken from 1 Corinthians 12-15. Most of the Gospel Readings are from Luke 1-6. It would be helpful to read and pray through these chapters and catch some of the vision that they present to us.

SECOND SUNDAY OF THE YEAR

THEME
The Church's Bridegroom.

PRAYER FOCUS
Show us the way to peace in the world.
Question: Is 'Peace in the world' an ambition of your's? How can
you make it more so?

READINGS

1) Isaiah 62:1-5
You are to be a crown of splendour in the hand of the Lord.
Question: How do you need to grow in a spirit of joy
and adventure?

2) Response (to Psalm 95)
Proclaim the wonders of the Lord among all the peoples.
Pray this response silently and aloud until you catch the spirit
of it.

3) Corinthians 12:4-11
There is a variety of gifts but always the same spirit.
Question: What are three of the main gifts you have for bringing
life to others? How do you use these?

4) John 2:1-12
Jesus said: 'Fill the jars with water',
and they filled them to the brim.
Question: How do you measure out your love for others?

QUESTIONS FOR ACTION

For Married Couples: In what special way could you be romantic
in your love this week?

For Others: How can you take an active part in church unity
week?

THIRD SUNDAY OF THE YEAR

THEME
The Law of the Lord.

PRAYER FOCUS
That our efforts in the name of your son
may bring unity and peace.
Question: How can you make this prayer more than a formality?

READINGS

1) Nehemiah 8:2-6; 8-10
Do not be sad; the joy of the Lord is your stronghold.
Question: Is your experience of religion mainly sad or joyful?
Why?

2) Response (to Psalm 18)
Your words are spirit, Lord, and they are life.
Pray this until you know you believe it in your heart.

3) 1 Corinthians 12:12-30
You together are Christ's body;
each of you is a different part of it.
Question: How can you help to continue the spirit of church
unity week in your own community?

4) Luke 1:1-4; 4:14-21
This text is being fulfilled today even as you listen.
Question: How aware are you of the living presence of Christ?

QUESTIONS FOR ACTION

For Married Couples: How can you keep a smile on the face of
your wife/husband this week?

For Others: With whom could you reconcile in some way this
week?

FOURTH SUNDAY OF THE YEAR

THEME
The struggle of faith.

PRAYER FOCUS
Help us to love you with all our hearts
and to love all people as you love them.
Question: Does this prayer excite you or leave you cold? Why?

READINGS

1) Jeremiah 1:4-5, 17-19
Before I formed you in the womb I knew you.
Question: Do you ever think about your own beginnings?
About the mystery of yourself?

2) Response (to Psalm 70)
My lips will tell of your help.
Pray this response, thinking of the times you experienced God's
help in your life.

3) 1 Corinthians 12:31-13, 13
Be ambitious for the higher gifts.
Question: What are your ambitions for life? How do they have to
change and develop?

4) Luke 4:21-30
No prophet is ever accepted in his own country.
Question: Are you ever uncertain about Christ?

QUESTIONS FOR ACTION

For Married Couples: Is there anything you need forgiveness for
from your wife/husband?

For Others: Is there anything you need forgiveness for from
someone close to you?

FIFTH SUNDAY OF THE YEAR

THEME
Christ makes us his apostles.

PRAYER FOCUS
Watch over your family and keep us safe in your care.
Question: How much do you really need God in your life?

READINGS

1) Isaiah 6:1-8
I Answered: 'Here I am, send me.'
Question: Do you feel reluctant about getting fully involved in
the work of God's kingdom? Why?

2) Response (to Psalm 137)
Before the angels I will bless you, O Lord.
Pray this response aloud and silently so as to feel the joy of it.

3) 1 Corinthians 15:1-11
What matters is that I preach what they preach.
Question: How do you need to grow in your love for the
Church?

4) Luke 5:1-11
'Do not be afraid.'
Question: What fears do you have about following Christ fully?

QUESTIONS FOR ACTION

For Married Couples: What in your life would you most like
to talk to your wife/husband about?
How could you do it this week?

For Others: To whom could you talk about Christ's love this
week?

SIXTH SUNDAY OF THE YEAR

THEME
Our trust in the Lord.

PRAYER FOCUS
Help us to live in your presence.
Question: What prevents you from being aware of God's presence in daily living?

READINGS

1) Jeremiah 17:5-8
A blessing on the person who puts his trust in the Lord.
Question: What do you put your trust in for the future?

2) Response (to Psalm 1)
Happy the person who puts his trust in the Lord.
Pray this until there is no longer any reluctance to believe it.

3) 1 Corinthians 15:2; 16-20
If Christ raised from the dead is what has been preached…
Question: How does your faith in eternal life change your way of seeing life now?

4) Luke 6:17; 20-26
Happy are you who are poor. Alas for you who are rich.
Question: Is it difficult for you to accept this? Why?

QUESTIONS FOR ACTION

For Married Couples: How could you show trust in your wife/husband in a special way this week?

For Others: Think of something you own which would be difficult for you to give away. To whom could you give it this week?

SEVENTH SUNDAY OF THE YEAR

THEME
The love of our Father.

PRAYER FOCUS
Help us to be like your son in word and deed.
Question: How much do you want this for yourself?

READINGS

1) 1 Samuel 26:2; 7-9; 12-13; 22-23
The Lord repays everyone for his uprightness and loyalty.
Question: Who are some of the most upright and loyal people
you know.

2) Response (to Psalm 102)
The Lord is compassion and love.
Pray this response silently and aloud until you are
in touch with the wonder of it.

3) 1 Corinthians 15:45-49
The last Adam has become a life-giving spirit.
Question: How important is Christ for our world today?

4) Luke 6:27-38
Treat others as you would like them to treat you.
Question: How do you want others to treat you?

QUESTIONS FOR ACTION

For Married Couples: In what way could you try to understand
your wife/husband better this week?

For Others: Whom could you treat with special kindness this
week?

EIGHTH SUNDAY OF THE YEAR

THEME
Praise and thanksgiving.

PRAYER FOCUS
Guide the course of world events and give your church
the joy and peace of serving you in freedom.
Question: How can this prayer be answered in the world in
which you live?

READINGS

1) Ecclesiasticus 27:4-7
The test of a person is in his conversation.
Question: What does that say about you?

2) Response (to Psalm 91)
It is good to give you thanks, O Lord.
Pray this repeatedly, recognising how much you have to be
thankful for.

3) 1 Corinthians 15:54-58
Let us thank God for giving us the victory
through our Lord Jesus Christ.
Question: How does this statement make you feel?

4) Luke 6:39-45
A person's words flow out from what is in his heart.
Question: What do your words tell you about yourself?

QUESTIONS FOR ACTION

For Married Couples: What three things are you most grateful to
your wife/husband for in the last two months?
How can you show it?

For Others: Who is closest to you in your life? How can you
show your appreciation to them this week?

SECTION 3

Lent

Introduction

'You must not put the Lord your God to the test'

Lent is a special time to stand back a little bit and look at the true quality of our lives, our loves, our hopes and dreams, our future and our past. There are all kinds of things we can look at and look for. Maybe this year it would be particularly helpful to look at how much of life is wasted by playing games. I am not thinking about sport, which can be very healthy. I am thinking about the unhealthy posturing that is so easy to get into. And it is such a waste of happiness.

Power game

The Original Sin was: not letting God be God. And people are still at it! In our world there is so much pretending to be important because of the position in government or business or media or Church etc. that a person holds. Lent is a great time to put all that into proper perspective and to simply rejoice in being alive and to know that every person is important.

Wealth mania

Week after week people are putting their trust for the future on winning the Lotto. And week after week they go away disappointed. Our society is quickly forming people into being graspers for all they can get. Lent is a time for learning again the art of giving to others, and the freedom that this gives.

Pleasure pursuits

People have a right to enjoy living. But when pleasure becomes the purpose of life, as it would seem to be for many people, it leads to all kinds of abuses of others. Pain is also a normal part of life. There is physical pain that has to be borne gracefully. People experience pain in relationships as a necessary part of growth and have to be able to work through it towards proper love. And there is the pain of hurt in life that needs to be healed by forgiveness. When pleasure is promoted for us as the only thing in life, we give up when there is suffering of any kind, either by looking for a new relationship that won't hurt, by revenge that will hurt others, or by suicide that will take it all away. Lent is a time to restore the balance of life where we learn again and again to live the present moment to the full.

What's it all about?

Isn't it amazing the hours that are spent in pubs and at parties solving all the problems of the world? Isn't it equally amazing how many pages are taken up in newpapers every day, how many chat-shows on TV and radio, endlessly pontificating on life? So much of it is like children's games played out by adults and with far less real interest. Lent is a time for reflecting again on what life is really about. We are ultimately people who desperately need God to show us our true dignity and worth. Human life can only be truly lived in love and compassion and concern. Life can only be enjoyed when it is placed in God's creative plan in which we can know our smallness and realise our greatness. It is in the death and resurrection of Christ that we come to see how much we are treasured and for what we are destined. These six weeks can be a time of real hope.

Some Features

The Gospel Readings are mostly from Luke 4-15. These chapters could be an excellent source of reflection and prayer right through the six weeks of Lent.

ASH WEDNESDAY

THEME
Repent and believe.

PRAYER FOCUS
Make this day holy by our self-denial.

READINGS

1) Joel 2:12-18

2) Response (to Psalm 50)
Have mercy on us O Lord for we have sinned.

3) 2 Corinthians 5:20-6, 2

4) Matthew 6:1-6; 16-18

POINTS

1) Ash Wednesday sets the scene for Lent. It is a special season of renewal for the Church each year. The key to the renewal is found in the second reading today: 'We are ambassadors for Christ. We beg you not to neglect the grace of God that you have received.'

2) Nothing positive happens unless we want it and unless we put ourselves out and go after it.

3) Giving to others, Self-discipline, Prayer, are identified as the three essential ways of accomplishing this renewal.

QUESTIONS

With what person or group will you be particularly generous with your possessions over the next six weeks?

How will you devote more time to prayer over the next six weeks?

What act of self-discipline will you undertake for the next six weeks?

FIRST SUNDAY OF LENT

THEME
Jesus is Lord.

PRAYER FOCUS
Teach us to reflect your son's death and resurrection
in our lives.
Question: In what ways do you need greater freedom to love
and to let yourself be loved?

READINGS

1) Deuteronomy 26:4-10
'My father was a wandering Aramean.'
Question: What are your origins? How do you feel about them?

2) Response (to Psalm 90)
Be with me O Lord, in my distress.
Pray this until you can know your need of God.

3) Romans 10:8-13
By believing from the heart you are made righteous.
Question: What are the origins of your faith? How do you feel
about this?

4) Luke 4:1-13
Jesus was led by the spirit through the wilderness
and was tempted there by the devil for forty days.
Question: What are some of your temptations in life?

QUESTIONS FOR ACTION

For Married Couples: What are the origins of your married love?
Recall these this week.

For Others: How could you honour your parents, even those
who have died, in a special way this week?

SECOND SUNDAY OF LENT

THEME
The Lord in whom we put our faith.

PRAYER FOCUS
Enlighten us with your word
Question: How open are you to learning and growing?

READINGS

1) Genesis 15:5-12; 17-18
Abraham put his faith in the Lord.
Question: In what ways are you ever arrogant about things?

2) Response (to Psalm 26)
The Lord is my light and my help.
Pray this until you can know his presence with you.

3) Philippians 3:17-4, 1
For us, our homeland is in heaven.
Question: Do you believe this? What does it mean to you?

4) Luke 9:28-36
'Master, it is wonderful for us to be here.'
Question: Is that your experience of the presence of Christ?
How do you need to let it develop?

QUESTIONS FOR ACTION
For Married Couples: How can you bring a sense of wonder and
joy to your wife/husband this week?
For Others: To whom could you bring special joy and happiness
this week?

THIRD SUNDAY OF LENT

THEME
The Lord of compassion and love.

PRAYER FOCUS
When we are discouraged by our weakness,
give us confidence in your love.
Question: Do you ever feel discouraged? When?

READINGS

1) Exodus 3:1-8; 13-15
'Take off your shoes, for the place where you stand
is holy ground.
Question: Do you ever have a sense of awe and wonder about
where you are, especially at home?

2) Response (to Psalm 102)
The Lord is compassion and love.
Pray this until you can feel the healing power of it.

3) Corinthians 10:1-6; 10-12
The person who thinks he is safe must be careful
that he does not fall.
Question: What does this mean to you? Can you apply it to
yourself?

4) Luke 13:1-9
It may bear fruit next year
Question: What are your hopes and ambitions for your parish
community?

QUESTIONS FOR ACTION

For Married Couples: What are your ambitions for your
marriage? Share these this week.

For Others: Do you know anyone who is discouraged?
What can you do for them this week?

FOURTH SUNDAY OF LENT

THEME
The Lord who welcomes sinners.

PRAYER FOCUS
Let us hasten towards Easter with the eagerness
of faith and love.
Question: How do you need to grow in eagerness about the
things of God?

READINGS

1) Joshua 5:9-12
'Today I have taken the shame of Egypt away from you.'
Question: In what ways are we still like slaves in our world
today?

2) Response (to Psalm 33)
Taste and see that the Lord is good.
Pray this until you can feel a real hunger for the Lord.

3) 2 Corinthians 5:17-21
The appeal that we make in Christ's name is:
Be reconciled to God.
Question: In what ways do you need to be reconciled to God?

4) Luke 15:1-3; 11-32
'This man', they said, 'welcomes sinners and eats with them'.
Question: Do you ever write people off and refuse to have
anything to do with them?

QUESTIONS FOR ACTION

For Married Couples: What annoys you about your wife/
husband? How can you work at getting over this, this week?

For Others: How could you help those who are working for the
marginalised around you?

FIFTH SUNDAY OF LENT

THEME
The Lord who has wiped away our sins.

PRAYER FOCUS
Inspire us by his love, guide us by his example.
Question: What do you need to look for in this prayer?

READINGS

1) Isaiah 43:16-21
See, I am doing a new deed, even now it comes to light;
can you not see it?
Question: In what ways are you tied to the past?

2) Response (to Psalm 125)
What marvels the Lord worked for us! Indeed we were glad.
Pray this until you can feel the power of it.

3) Philippians 3:8-14
I forget the past and I strain ahead for what is still to come.
Question: What are your hopes and dreams for your faith and
life?

4) John 8:1-11
'If there is one of you who has not sinned, let him be the first to
throw a stone at her.'
Question: In what ways are you ever self-righteous
and judgemental of others?

QUESTIONS FOR ACTION

For Married Couples: Is there anything in the past for which
you haven't fully forgiven your wife/husband?
Work at it this week.

For Others: Is there anything in the past for which you need to
forgive someone in your life? Work at it this week.

HOLY WEEK

THEME
Through death to life.

POINTS TO PONDER

1) In our life of faith this is a very special week. We call it Holy Week. That means that we see it as totally different from every other week of our year. How different is it in practice?

2) We often say that Christmas is cluttered up with glitter and commercialism. Holy Week is equally distracted from by pressure for holidays, getting to the sun etc..

3) We make Holy Week very special by:
(a) Taking a lot more time than normal for prayer.
(b) Being more committed than usual to being part of our local community.
(c) Sharing, especially in our families, our story of faith, our roots, our journey.

4) Holy Week is like a call to the whole Church throughout the world to go on retreat together, using all the resources we have for making Christ present in our world so that together we can shout out his resurrection at Easter, a shout that will shake the ends of the earth.

5) Like the life of the Church generally, the success of Holy Week depends so much on how each of us personally, and as communities, takes our part fully, freely, joyfully.

SECTION 4

Passion Sunday - Easter Sunday

PASSION SUNDAY (PALM SUNDAY)

PART 1

THEME
Hosanna to the son of David

PRAYER FOCUS
May we honour you every day by living always in him.

READING

Luke 19:28-40
The whole group of disciples began to praise God joyfully
at the top of their voices.

QUESTIONS

Why is our practice of faith in Jesus often so low-key?

What prevents you from being more outgoing and joyful
in living your faith?

PART 2

FOCUS
Crucify him, crucify him

READINGS

1) Isaiah 50:4-7
I set my face like flint. I know I shall not be shamed.

2) Response (to Psalm 21)
My God, My God, why have you forsaken me?

3) Philippians 2:6-11
God raised him high.

4) Luke 22:14-23, 56

QUESTIONS

Have you ever been betrayed or hurt by someone you loved?
Are you free from that now?

HOLY THURSDAY

THEME
The extent of God's love.

PRAYER FOCUS
That we may find the fulness of life and love.

READINGS

1) Exodus 12:1-8; 11-14

2) Response (to Psalm 115)
The blessing cup that we bless is a communion
with the blood of Christ.

3) 1 Corinthians 11:23-26

4) John 13:1-15
Do you understand what I have done to you?

QUESTIONS

How aware are you of how much you are loved by God?
How do you need to grow in that awareness?

How will you show your wife/husband how precious
s/he is to you today?

GOOD FRIDAY

THEME
Christ has died.

PRAYER FOCUS
Make us holy and watch over us always.

READINGS

1) Isaiah 52:13-53:12

2) Response (to Psalm 30)
Father, into your hands I commend my spirit.

3) John 18:1-19, 42
I am thirsty.

PRAYERS OF INTERCESSION

That the death of Christ may bring life to all people.

QUESTIONS

What would you want to say to your wife/husband or some
loved one at their death? Say it today!

In what ways does our world need the salvation of Christ?

HOLY SATURDAY

THEME
A day of waiting.

PRAYER FOCUS
Renew us in mind and body to give you whole-hearted service.

READINGS

Genesis 1:1-2, 22:1-18; Exodus 14:15, 1; Isaiah 54:5-14, 55:1-11;
Baruch 3:9-15; 32-4, 4; Ezechiel 36:16-17a; 18-28
In these readings creation and history are brought together
to proclaim the wonders of God.

2) Romans 6:3-11

3) Luke 24:1-12
Why look among the dead for someone who is alive?

QUESTION
In what ways do you need to open out from a small world
into the vast world of God's love and creation?

EASTER SUNDAY

THEME
A day of celebration.

PRAYER FOCUS
Raise us up and renew our lives by the spirit that is within us.

READINGS

1) Acts 10:34; 37-43.
We are his witnesses.

2) Response (to Psalm 117)
This day was made by the Lord; we rejoice and are glad.

3) Colossians 3:1-4
Let your thoughts be on heavenly things.

4) John 20:1-9
He must be raised from the dead.

QUESTIONS

In what ways do you need greater freedom in your life?

In what ways can you bring greater freedom to your
wife/husband, family and other loved ones?

Easter 2 - Pentecost

Introduction

Receive the Holy Spirit

This section of the Church's liturgical year leads us into Pentecost Sunday, the day when the Holy Spirit filled the followers of Jesus and gave them a new sense of purpose. However, on the first day of this section, Jesus is already urging us: 'Receive the Holy Spirit'. We are once again at the heart of the mystery of God's desire for us and our reluctance to let go.

A paradox

We are a people who have already received the Holy Spirit. God's Spirit has filled the Church since that first Pentecost day. We individually received that same Spirit on the day of our Confirmation. How can we receive him again? That is precisely the paradox and the problem. We have to acknowledge our need of the Spirit and our possession of the Spirit at the same time. And our need is that we simply settle down into repeating religious actions rather than being on fire with love and hope and a real sense of purpose for our world.

What are the signs?

The gifts of the Holy Spirit are good testing points for our need to be open to a fresh outpouring again this year:

1. *Wisdom:* How easily we settle for the superficial wisdom of life and dress it up to make it look good. The real wisdom that is on offer is the wisdom of a little child who is in awe at the wonders of life. How close are we to that, personally and as a Church?

2. *Understanding:* So much of life is spent in self-protection. A sign of this is how we so easily depend on structures to save us. True understanding is seen in a person or a community that is free to love, to hope, to have compassion, ready to forgive. How badly we need the Holy Spirit to move us to those points.

3. *Counsel:* A good counsellor is not one who solves our problems but one who can lead us into the true centre of our lives. The gift of counsel helps us to know that the only reality is God, the only true life we have is Christ, our only homeland is heaven. Life for countless people and for the Church can so easily become a succession of problems being solved, where we cope with life rather than live it from within. We need God's Spirit to set us free.

4. *Fortitude:* Original sin is still being born in us as we try to be God rather than creature, someone who has everything by gift. It comes from within us as individuals. It rises also from the heart of the Church. It is only when we are in awe at our own utter weakness and fragility that we can acknowledge our true strength, the extreme love of God for us. The Spirit is given to bring us there and to set us free from our need to dominate life, others, God. Come, Holy Spirit.

5. *Knowledge:* One of the major mistakes of life is to think that what we know is all there is to know. There is such a vast, wonderful world beyond ourselves to conquer. This is true of the physical world. It is even more true of the spiritual world of the human person. The Holy Spirit keeps urging us out of our own little world of conceit and limited knowledge into the large world of God's magnificent creation in us and around us.

6. *Piety:* 'Where you treasure is, there will your heart be also.' What we value most in life determines how we live. So much selfishness and self-preoccupation would indicate where our true values are as individuals and as a Church. It is only the Spirit of God that can blast us out of the hardness of heart into taking on the new heart of affection for God and for one another. The gift of piety, of submission in humility to the truth of life, is a great need in us today. Receive the Holy Spirit.

7. *Fear of the Lord:* 'Do not be afraid' is the most repeated sentence in the Scriptures. Fear is identified as the greatest obstacle to life and to love. Yet fear continues to be used as a weapon in our relationships with God and with one another. God's Holy Spirit leads us to the deepest truth of our lives, the passionate, intimate, personal love of God. That same Spirit brings us to the point of falling in love with God so that our whole lives get caught up in that relationship. The only fear is that of someone who is madly in love.

Receive the Holy Spirit

Jesus speaks these words right through these weeks, urging us to take them seriously and let ourselves go, to all that he has to offer us. We cannot afford to simply play games of religion with this call.

SECOND SUNDAY OF EASTER

THEME
The living one.

PRAYER FOCUS
Renew your gifts of life within us.

READINGS

1) Acts 5:12-16
The people were loud in their praise.
Question: What's needed for the Church today to be a source of
praise for others?

2) Response (to Psalm 117)
Give thanks to the Lord for he is good, for his love has no end.
Pray this response until you feel the wonder of his love.

3) Apocalypse 1:9-13; 17-19
Do not be afraid … I am the living one.
Question: In what ways are you afraid of going further in your
faith and knowledge of Jesus?

4) John 20:19-31
'Unless I see … I refuse to believe.'
Question: What obstacles do you have to full faith in Christ and
his presence with you now?

QUESTIONS FOR ACTION

For Married Couples: What's needed for you to bring more life
into your marriage relationship?
What can you do about it this week?

For Others: To whom could you bring special joy this week?
How will you do it?

THIRD SUNDAY OF EASTER

THEME
'It is the Lord.'

PRAYER FOCUS
May we look forward to our resurrection
Question: Is that a desire of your's?

READINGS

1) Acts 5:27-32; 40-41
They were glad to have had the honour of suffering and
humiliation for the sake of his name.
Question: Have you ever experienced humiliation for the sake of
your faith?

2) Response (to Psalm 29)
I will praise you, Lord, you have rescued me.
Pray this response until you know its truth for you.

3) Apocalypse 5:11-14
Then I heard all creation crying – 'To the Lamb be all praise'
Question: How much in touch are you with the power that's in
creation?

4) John 21:1-19
'Come and have breakfast.'
Question: Is your knowledge of Jesus as real as that?

QUESTIONS FOR ACTION
For Married Couples: How could you make breakfast-time
special for your wife/husband this week?

For Others: How could you get more in touch with the wonders
of creation this week?

FOURTH SUNDAY OF EASTER

THEME
The Lamb will be our shepherd.

PRAYER FOCUS
Give us new strength through the courage of Christ
Question: How do you need new strength in your life?

READINGS

1) Acts 13:14; 43-52
The Jews, prompted by jealousy, contradicted everything
Paul said.
Question: How does jealousy disrupt your community today?

2) Response (to Psalm 99)
We are his people, the sheep of his flock.
Pray this response until you can be glad of it.

3) Apocalypse 7:9; 14-17
God will wipe away all tears from their eyes
Question: In what ways do you avoid suffering,
especially in regard to living out your faith?

4) John 10:27-30
The sheep that belong to me listen to my voice.
Question: When have you had a deep experience of being loved?
What was that like for you?

QUESTIONS FOR ACTION

For Married Couples: How could you make your wife/husband
feel specially loved this week?

For Others: Choose someone in your life whom you will praise
and affirm in special ways this week. How will you do it?

FIFTH SUNDAY OF EASTER

THEME
The new creation.

PRAYER FOCUS
Give us true freedom
Question: In what ways do you lack true freedom in yourself?

READINGS

1) Acts 14:21-27
They put fresh heart into the disciples
Question: How do you think others around you need fresh heart
in their faith? How can you contribute to this?

2) Response (to Psalm 144)
I will bless your name forever, O God, my king.
Pray this response aloud and in silence
until it comes from the heart.

3) Apocalypse 21:1-5
'Now I am making the whole of creation new', he said.
Question: Are you hopeful or sad about our world?

4) John 13:31-35
I give you a new commandment:- Love one another.
Question: Do you believe this is the most important thing in our
following of Christ.

QUESTIONS FOR ACTION

For Married Couples: How could you bring greater freedom to
your love-making this week?

For Others: How could you bring hope and confidence to
someone this week?

SIXTH SUNDAY OF EASTER

THEME
The radiant glory of God.

PRAYER FOCUS
Help us to celebrate our joy in the resurrection of Christ and to express in our lives the love we celebrate.
Question: What's needed so that you can live in joy this coming week?

READINGS

1)Acts 15:1-2; 22-29
It has been decided not to saddle you with any burden beyond these essentials.
Question: What unnecessary burdens are in the Church today?

2) Response (to Psalm 66)
Let the people praise you, O Lord,
Let all the peoples praise you.
Pray this fervently until you want it to happen.

3) Apocalypse 21:10-14; 22-23
The city was lit by the radiant glory of God.
Question: Do you ever get excited by faith? When?

4) John 14:23-29
Peace I bequeath to you, my own peace I leave you.
Question: What disturbs peace in your heart, in your world?

QUESTIONS FOR ACTION

For Married Couples: How could you bring a sense of deep peace to your wife/husband this week?

For Others: What will you do to encourage peace among individuals or in society this week?

SEVENTH SUNDAY OF EASTER

THEME
The spirit and the bride, the Church.

PRAYER FOCUS
That we may always know that Christ is with us.
Question: Do you want that knowledge? What are you willing to do to get it?

READINGS

1) Acts 7:55-60
Lord do not hold this sin against them
Question: What is your attitude to those who harm you?

2) Response (to Psalm 96)
The Lord is King, most high above all the earth.
Pray this response until you can experience something of the wonder of the Lord.

3) Apocalypse 22:12-14; 16-17; 20
Then let all who are thirsty come
Question: Are you satisfied with what you have or do you thirst for more of life?

4) John 17:20-26
May they be so completely one that the world will realise.
Question: Answering this prayer of Jesus is our main way of following him. Do you believe this? Why?/Why not?

QUESTIONS FOR ACTION
For Married Couples: What will you do to grow in unity with each other this week?

For Others: How could you help your parish to be more a community this week?

PENTECOST

THEME
Empowered by the Holy Spirit.

PRAYER FOCUS
Let your spirit continue to work in the world through us.
Question: Do you really want that? How much?

READINGS

1) Acts 2:1-11
We hear them preaching in our own language
about the marvels of God.
Question: What do people in your life hear from you?

2) Response (to Psalm 103)
Send forth your spirit, O Lord, and renew the face of the earth.
Pray this for as long as it takes to really want it.

3) 1 Corinthians 12:3-7; 12-13
There is a variety of gifts, but always the same spirit.
Question: What gifts do you have for others?
How do you use them?

4) John 20:19-23
As the father sent me, so am I sending you
Question: Are you willing to take your full place in the mission
of the Church? How do you see it?

QUESTIONS FOR ACTION

For Married Couples: What are three of the best gifts your
wife/husband has right now?
How will you communicate that this week?

For Others: Choose two or three people in your life.
What are three of the best gifts each of them has?
How will you tell them this week?

Note

After Pentecost, go to Trinity Sunday. After that, you may have to go back into some of the later Sundays of section 2, depending on the date of Easter in this particular year. You then follow the sequence of Sundays through until the end of the year.

Trinity Sunday - 15th Sunday of the Year

Introduction

Who is my neighbour?

After the last few months of Lent, Easter, Pentecost and all the special feasts of the Church, we now enter into what is called Ordinary Time. The temptation is to regard this as meaning 'business as usual' and give a great sigh of relief that all the intensity of faith is over for another few months at least. If we reflect on this next section of the Church's liturgical year we see clearly that it is no time to free-wheel. In these past few months we have been put in touch with the vast resources that are at our disposal, especially the new life of Christ and God's own Holy Spirit. In the weeks ahead we are opened up to where Christ wants us to go – into a knowledge of the true God and towards a real love for one another. Christ's central message is that the only way to true human life is to love God with our whole heart, our whole soul, our whole mind, our whole strength and to love our neighbour as ourselves.

Who is our God?

On the First Sunday of this section we celebrate the Feast of the Most Holy Trinity. It is total act of faith because our reason cannot reach anywhere near it. But it is an act of faith in the word of Jesus that our God is Father, Son, Spirit. All we can do is submit ourselves in awe to this God who, though totally complete, is weak with love for us. We have simply to let this knowledge take us over and let ourselves be pursued by this wonderful lover and find ourselves taken out of our own tiny little worlds into the vast world of the love of our God.

Who is my neighbour?

This is the question that surfaces on the last Sunday of this section and indicates the second place that Jesus wants us to go – towards one another in love. Again we reach towards this point of each other as a total act of faith. Reason cannot really tell us much about one another because our likes and dislikes get in the way. Faith points us towards the utter dignity and worth that we have to reverence in action and not just in words. Who is my neighbour? This question was asked in self-defence. Jesus pulled down the defences by telling a story of someone in need, a man left for dead, and everyone passing him by for their own good reasons. Everyone, that is, except someone who had nothing to lose but his own possessions, the good Samaritan. That is our story and we need to let it open us up to freedom of spirit.

Blocks to freedom

1. *Selfishness:* The first great block that we have to deal with is our own selfishness. Today there is such a strong sense of 'I feel like it, therefore I do it'. This is the cause of so much misery in broken marriages, divided families, unhappy homes. Our neighbour is first the person that is closest to us and we have to attend that person with love. This always means change in ourselves, letting go of our own selfish needs and doing what is best for our loved ones and for our relationships with them.

2. *Prejudice:* We are so full of them that we don't even know we have them most of the time! Prejudice keeps us at a distance from most people. We don't even notice so may of those around us because we have written them off in our own minds and hearts. There is prejudice between women and men that are cultural as well as personal. There is prejudice between different classes of people that is social as well as personal and there is prejudice between churches that is spiritual as well as personal. Prejudice is a major crippling force in our following of Christ towards one another.

3. *Preoccupation:* If you ever watch people in a crowd you will see the power of preoccupation on them. If it's a crowd of total strangers as in a shopping centre or busy city street you will see people almost walking through each other. So many look as if the burdens of the world are on their shoulders! If it's a crowd at a family or social gathering people are preoccupied with how they look, how they sound, how they are noticed. Preoccupation ties us up into ourselves so that we cannot notice or listen to the amazing beauty that is in ourselves and every person we meet.

Who is my neighbour? We'll never know until we let go of our
own tiny place and reach out.

Special Features
The prayers of the Mass these Sundays are searching for freedom for us. Make inner freedom to love a pursuit during this
time. Most of the Second Readings are from St Paul's Letter to
the Galatians 2–6. Most of the Gospel Readings are from Luke
7–10. It would be good to read these chapters as a piece during
this time.

TRINITY SUNDAY

THEME
Glory to the Father, Son and Holy Spirit.

PRAYER FOCUS
Help us to worship you by proclaiming and living our faith
Question: Do people generally think of 'worship' as words
spoken or as life lived? Do you?

READINGS

1) Proverbs 8:22-31
The wisdom of God cries aloud, the Lord created me
when his purpose first unfolded.
Question: In what ways is life lived at a superficial level?

2) Response (to Psalm 8)
How great is your name, O Lord our God, through all the earth.
Pray this until you really want it to happen.

3) Romans 5:1-5
We can boast about our suffering?
Question: What is your attitude to suffering?

4) John 16:12-15
He will lead you to the complete truth.
Question: In what ways do you need to be more open to learning
and so to change?

QUESTIONS FOR ACTION

For Married Couples: In what part of your relationship do you
least understand your wife/husband? How can you work on
this during the coming week?

For Others: What special time could you take for prayer this
week?

NINTH SUNDAY OF THE YEAR

THEME
Go out to the whole world.

PRAYER FOCUS
Keep us from danger and provide for all our needs.
Question: How much room do you leave in your life for God to
answer that prayer?

READINGS

1) 1 Kings 8:41-43
That all the peoples of the earth may come to know your name.
Question: Is this an ambition of yours or do you never think of
it? Why/Why not?

2) Response (to Psalm 116)
Go out to the whole world and proclaim the good news.
Pray and reflect on this response until you want it to happen.

3) Galatians 1:1-2, 6-10
If anyone preaches a version of the good news different from
the one you have already heard, he/she is to be condemned.
Question: What is the heart of the good news for you?

4) Luke 7:1-10
I am not worthy to have you under my roof.
Question: Do you ever feel that way about the Lord? Explain.

QUESTIONS FOR ACTION

For Married Couples: How could you show your wife/husband
how special she/he is to you this week?

For Others: How could you encourage someone this week to get
more involved with Christ in his Church?

TENTH SUNDAY OF THE YEAR

THEME
God has visited his people.

PRAYER FOCUS
Send your Spirit to teach us your truth
and guide our actions in your way of peace.
Question: Do you really want that prayer answered
for yourself and for your community?

READINGS

1) 1 Kings 17:17-24
'Look,' Elijah said, 'your son is alive.'
Question: Do you believe in miracles? Why/Why not?

2) Response (to Psalm 29)
I will praise you, Lord, you have rescued me.
Pray this response, reflecting on any times it may have been
true in your own life or the life of someone you know.

3) Galations 1:11-19
God called me through his grace
and chose to reveal his Son in me.
Question: Do you believe that statement is true about you?

4) Luke 7:11-17
'Do not cry,' Jesus said,
and he gave the young man to his mother.
Question: Have you ever experienced the healing power of
Christ in your life? If so, when/how?

QUESTIONS FOR ACTION

For Married Couples: When have you felt most in love with your
wife/husband? Relive those times this week.

For Others: Do you know anyone who is very ill at present?
How could you comfort them this week?

ELEVENTH SUNDAY OF THE YEAR

THEME
The forgiving Christ.

PRAYER FOCUS
Help us to follow Christ and to live according to your will.
Question: What do you need to do so that this prayer
can be answered in your life?

READINGS

1) 2 Samuel 12:7-10; 13
'The Lord, for his part, forgives your sin. You are not to die.'
Question: People have lost a sense of sin today.
How true is that statement? How true is it about you?

2) Response (to Psalm 31)
Forgive, Lord, the guilt of my sin.
Pray this response slowly, searching for peace.

3) Galatians 2:16; 19-21
I live now not with my own life but with the life of
Christ who lives in me.
Question: How do you feel as you think about that statement
in relation to yourself?

4) Luke 7:36-8:3
It is the person who is forgiven little that shows little love.
Question: How difficult is it for you to admit when you are
wrong and to ask forgiveness? How can you change?

QUESTIONS FOR ACTION
For Married Couples: What do you need to ask forgiveness for
from your wife/husband? Ask her/him if necessary!

For Others: Is there anyone whom you need to forgive? Work on
it this week.

TWELFTH SUNDAY OF THE YEAR

THEME
He gave his life for us.

PRAYER FOCUS
Give us an unfailing respect for your name.
Question: What does that mean to you?

READINGS

1) Zechariah 12:10-11
I will pour out a spirit of kindness and prayer
Question: In what ways do you need that spirit?

2) Response (to Psalm 62)
For you my soul is thirsting, O God, my God.
Pray this response until you know your need of God.

3) Galatians 3:26-29
All of you are one in Christ Jesus
Question: In what ways do you need to be more one with your
family, your parish community?

4) Luke 9:18-24
Anyone who loses his life for my sake will save it.
Question: How seriously do you take that promise of Christ?
Why?

QUESTIONS FOR ACTION

For Married Couples: How could you have a greater spirit of
kindness towards your wife/husband this week?

For Others: To whom could you be specially kind this week so as
to make a difference in their lives?

THIRTEENTH SUNDAY OF THE YEAR

THEME
The Lord we serve.

PRAYER FOCUS
Free us from darkness and keep us in the radiance of your truth.
Question: In what ways do you/we need to be freed
from darkness?

READINGS

1) 1 Kings 19:16; 19-21
Have I done anything to you?
Question: In what ways do you hold back from serving God?

2) Response (to Psalm 15)
O Lord, it is you who are my portion
Pray this response until you are filled with it.

3) Galatians 5:1; 13-18
You were called to liberty.
Question: In what ways do you need greater freedom to love?

4) Luke 9:51-62
No one who looks back is fit for the kingdom of God
Question: What fears do you find in yourself in regard to
following Christ fully?

QUESTIONS FOR ACTION

For Married Couples: What fears do you have in giving yourself
fully to your wife/husband? Share these this week.

For Others: Is there anyone with whom you are angry
at present? How can you let go of this, this week?

FOURTEENTH SUNDAY OF THE YEAR

THEME
Christ, our peace.

PRAYER FOCUS
Free us from sin and bring us to the joy that lasts forever
Question: How does sin destroy joy and peace?

READINGS

1) Isaiah 66:10-14
To his servants the Lord will reveal his hand.
Question: Peace is the Lord's desire. How possible is it?

2) Response (to Psalm 65)
Cry out with joy to God all the earth.
Pray this response until you want it to happen.

3) Galatians 6:14-18
I want no more trouble from anybody after this.
Question: Why do people cause trouble for each other in family
and parish life today?

4) Luke 10:1-12; 17-20
The harvest is rich but the labourers are few
Question: In what ways can you personally and as a family
become more involved in bringing peace and hope to others?

QUESTIONS FOR ACTION

For Married Couples: How can you make this week enjoyable for
your wife/husband?

For Others: What can you do this week to promote peace at
family and community level?

FIFTEENTH SUNDAY OF THE YEAR

THEME
His word is near.

PRAYER FOCUS
May we reject what is contrary to the gospel
Question: What will this mean for you in the week ahead?

READINGS

1) Deuteronomy 30:10-14
The word is in your mouth and in your heart
Question: What does this mean to you?

2) Response (to Psalm 68)
Seek the Lord, you who are poor, and your hearts will revive.
Pray this response until you experience the hope it brings.

3) Colossians 1:15-20
The Church is his body, he is its head.
Question: How do you experience the close presence of Christ?

4) Luke 10:25-37
'Who is my neighbour?'
Question: In what ways do you put off fulfilling your
responsibilities towards people in your life?

QUESTIONS FOR ACTION

For Married Couples: In what particular ways will your
wife/husband need your love and care in the week ahead?

For Others: Who will most need your help and care in the week
ahead? How will you respond?

16th - 21st Sunday
of the Year

Introduction

Will there be only a few saved?

Every now and again someone promotes the idea that 'outside the Church there is no salvation', and the same people usually would give you the strong impression that inside the Church it is almost impossible also! The question 'will there be only a few saved?' is found on the 21st Sunday of the Year, the liturgy to which this section is leading. It challenges our whole idea of God, of ourselves, of what life is about, of where we are going.

Gospel truth

One of the lovely features of the gospels is that Jesus did not have any great trouble in being with and accepting what we would call sinners – prostitutes, adulterers, thieves, murderers. He didn't in any way condone their action. But he always had great compassion as he said things like 'go and do not sin any more', 'today you will be with me in paradise'.

The other side of this – and there always is another side! – was that Jesus had a lot of trouble with the good people, those who were virtuous, hard-working, law-abiding, self-righteous. Most of his energy seemed to be spent on them, trying to help them into freedom to worship God rather than themselves. That is still the struggle that Jesus has among us.

Hypocrites

A hypocrite is not just someone who doesn't live up to his/her word, to what he/she believes. That's ordinary human weakness. That's what being a sinner is. We are all guilty and we all need forgiveness. A hypocrite is one who doesn't really believe what he/she says, is not willing to be changed by God's Spirit, demands the right to be in control. A hypocrite is basically one who, while professing faith in God, worships himself or herself, or some system or belief or way of life. We, the Church, are always in danger of the condemnation that Jesus spoke to the scribes and pharisees: 'You hypocrites, you brood of vipers, you whited sepulchres, all shiny on the outside and inside full of dead people's bones.' We are forever making ourselves, our doctrines, our way, the centre of our faith, the source of our salvation, rather than Jesus who is Lord and who brings us into the freedom of God's love.

Steps to salvation

Week by week this section of the Church's liturgical year helps us to see what's needed in order to face the question for ourselves: Will there be only a few saved?

1. *Rid yourself of self-righteousness.* We so easily get so satisfied with ourselves that we dare take on the role of judge of others. Scandals get known about others and we move in on them in our conversations and actions because we are not like that. People's failures begin to show and we pull the holes of their lives even wider because we are so good. When we judge others we are making ourselves like God and we fall flat on our faces.

2. *Learn to trust God and to pray for all that you need.* It is wonderful for us to know God but we hope we will never really need him! We spend our lives trying to make sure of everything for ourselves. Our concentration is on having everything we need now and security for the future. But life is too fragile for that to be its aim and purpose. In our all-out efforts to make sure for ourselves, we are playing at being God and our efforts are futile.

3. *Practical forgiveness.* How much human energy is spent and wasted on quarrels, hurts, revenge, demanding justice. Unforgiveness keeps us rooted in the past. The result is that we are not free to live fully in the present. Anger over hurts makes us take it out on others, even people who have had no part in those hurts. Those closest to us suffer the most because we are not able to be fully for them. Revenge is a demand to have the power of God because only he has the right to truly judge. It destroys our spirit and our joy.

4. *Get your priorities right.* People usually go where they are looking! Where are you looking right now in your own life? Are you

looking towards yourself? That's where you will end up. Are you looking at hopelessness? That's what will take you over. Begin looking at life, full life now and eternal life. The only way to these is love of God with our whole hearts and love of one another. There is simply no other way. We have the word of God on that.

5. *Make Jesus your hope of salvation.* Even among good practising Catholics there is an awful reluctance to talk about or admit Christ. There is a crying need for inner freedom to let him take over our lives so that we may be alive and joyful, at peace with our God and with one another.

Some Features

These Sundays are another opportunity for us individually, and as a people, to sort ourselves out. There is so much on offer to us. We accept so little. Read Luke 10-13 and catch the spirit that is in this section. We will journey more freely with our Saviour.

SIXTEENTH SUNDAY OF THE YEAR

THEME
Jesus, our friend.

PRAYER FOCUS
Make us ever eager to serve you in faith, hope and love
Question: What helps you in/prevents you from being 'eager' to
serve God at present?

READINGS

1) Genesis 18:1-10
Kindly do not pass your servant by
Question: In what ways do you let the Lord pass you by?

2) Response (to Psalm 14)
Lord, who shall be admitted to your tent?
Pray this response until you can know the answer for yourself.

3) Colossians 1:24-28
The mystery is Christ among you, your hope of glory.
Question: How much does Christ mean to you?

4) Luke 10:38-42
You worry and fret about so many things.
Question: What are some of your worries? How do these rule
your life?

QUESTIONS FOR ACTION

For Married Couples: How could you be romantic for your
wife/husband this week?

For Others: Whom could you befriend in a special way this
week? How will you do it?

SEVENTEENTH SUNDAY OF THE YEAR

THEME
Lord, teach us to pray.

PRAYER FOCUS
Guide us to everlasting life
Question: How conscious are you of travelling towards
everlasting life?

READINGS

1) Genesis 18:20-32
'I am bold indeed to speak like this to my Lord.'
Question: How positive are you in what you ask of God?

2) Response (to Psalm 137)
On the day I called, you answered me, O Lord.
Pray this until you know the certainty of it.

3) Colossians 2:12-24
He has brought you to life with him. He has forgiven us
all our sins.
Question: In what ways do you experience new life in Christ?

4) Luke 11:1-13
Ask, and it will be given to you.
Question: What kind of things do you ask from God?
What kind of things do you receive?

QUESTIONS FOR ACTION
For Married Couples: How could you be 'bold' in reaching out in
love to your wife/husband this week?

For Others: How will you grow in prayer this week?

EIGHTEENTH SUNDAY OF THE YEAR

THEME
Our hardened hearts.

PRAYER FOCUS
Forgive our sins and restore us to life
Question: In what ways do you need forgiveness?

READINGS

1) Ecclesiastes 1:2; 2:21-23
What of all your laborious days, your cares of office,
your restless nights? This, too, is vanity.
Question: How do you experience the truth of this?

2) Response (to Psalm 94)
O that today you would listen to his voice!
Harden not your hearts.
Pray this until you find yourself at peace.

3) Colossians 3:1-5; 9-11
You have stripped off your old behaviour with your old self.
Question: How deep is your sense of faith in Christ?

4) Luke 12:13-21
Watch, and be on your guard against avarice of any kind.
Question: How do your possessions trap you?

QUESTIONS FOR ACTION

For Married Couples: What do you find most difficult to let go of
to your wife/husband? How will you work on it this week?

For Others: What will you give of your possessions to someone
in need during this coming week?

NINETEENTH SUNDAY OF THE YEAR

THEME
Ready for action.

PRAYER FOCUS
Increase your spirit within us.
Question: How do you need this prayer answered in your life?

READINGS

1) Wisdom 18:6-9
(They) Would share the same blessings and dangers alike.
Question: What things make you shy away from wanting to be
known as being part of the Church?

2) Response (to Psalm 32)
Happy are the people the Lord has chosen as his own.
Pray this until you know the truth of it for yourself.

3) Hebrews 11:1-2; 8-19
It was by faith that Abraham set out without knowing
where he was going.
Question: Do you find it difficult or easy to trust God? Why?

4) Luke 12:32-48
Where your treasure is, there will your heart be also.
Question: What do you treasure most in life? Why?

QUESTIONS FOR ACTION

For Married Couples: How can you anticipate some need in your
wife/husband this week?

For Others: Who would appreciate a contact from you this
week?

TWENTIETH SUNDAY OF THE YEAR

THEME
Victory with Christ.

PRAYER FOCUS
May we love you in all things and above all things and reach
the joy that is above all our imagining
Question: In what ways is your life hum-drum and boring?

READINGS

1) Jeremiah 38:4-6; 8-10
'The king is powerless against you.'
Question: When do you feel powerless? How do you act?

2) Response (to Psalm 39)
Lord, come to my aid.
Pray this until you know your need of God.

3) Hebrews 12:1-4
You will not give up for want of courage
Question: Do you ever feel like giving up?
When? What do you do?

4) Luke 12:49-53
I have come to bring fire to the earth, and how I wish it were
blazing already.
Question: How urgent are you about the things of God?
How does this need to grow in you?

QUESTIONS FOR ACTION

For Married Couples: What is your ambition for your marriage?
Share this with your spouse this week.

For Others: How can you help someone in serious need
this week?

TWENTY-FIRST SUNDAY OF THE YEAR

THEME
Saviour of all peoples.

PRAYER FOCUS
Make us one in mind and heart
Question: How much do you want that to happen?

READINGS

1) Isaiah 66:18-21
I am coming to gather the nations of every language.
Question: What do you think of this statement in the light of
today's world?

2) Response (to Psalm 116)
Go out to the whole world; proclaim the good news.
Pray this until you catch the spirit of hope in it.

3) Hebrews 12:5-7; 11-13
Suffering is part of your training.
Question: How do you handle suffering?

4) Luke 13:22-30
There are those now last who will be first, and those now first
who will be last.
Question: In what ways are you lazy in living your faith?

QUESTIONS FOR ACTION

For Married Couples: In what special way does your
wife/husband need to be loved in the week ahead?
How will you do it?

For Others: Whom do you most need to be reconciled? How will
you do it this week?

22nd - 27th Sunday
of the Year

Introduction

Increase our faith

This section leads the Church into that request from the disciples: 'Increase our faith.' We are often inclined to be content with what we have, and when we are we can be certain that it will grow less. These next few Sundays are an opportunity to stir ourselves out of our complacency and reach for a vibrant, living faith that can move mountains.

Enemies of faith

1. *Fear.* The single greatest enemy of faith is fear. This is how the Scriptures see it. They say that the sentence 'Do not be afraid' is found in the Scriptures 365 times. The greatest fear of all is that of how much it will cost us in terms of our own lives. The result of this fear is then that we set very low limits to faith and the practice of faith. We keep it well within our own control. As Catholics, we have reduced the practice of faith to going to Mass on Sunday, and then many search around for the quickest one! And we miss the point entirely. When we ask the Lord to increase our faith we need to let him set us free of our fears so that we can trust him.

2. *Possessions.* During the next four Sundays the Scriptures identify possessions as one of the major enemies of faith. On one of these days we hear Jesus say to his followers: 'None of you can be my disciple unless you give up all your possessions.' It's difficult even to read that – everything inside us reacts to it. We leave it there in the book and continue as we were!

Possessions are a very important part of life. But when they become the *objective* of life they destroy our freedom to live. The fact is that possessions posses us. The more we have the more of our attentions and energy is consumed in taking care of it all. In our society today we are getting more and more drawn into possessions. The advertising culture convinces us that if we don't have all that is on offer we cannot possibly be happy. When we get caught in that trap we lose sight of the Lord and have no great energy for following him. When we ask 'Increase our faith' we are asking him to free us from the power of our possessions.

3. *Pride.* As a word, pride is often thought of as meaning thinking highly of yourself. And that is not the case. In fact one of the greatest curses in human life is the poor self-image that most people have. Much of the escapism in our world is precisely from that. Pride means putting myself at the centre of my life and concerns. It means living as if all I have is mine rather than gift from God and others. It is about living as if I am my own creator and redeemer. We talk about looking after number one! That is the pride that prevents us from giving God his rightful place and it hinders us from making others really important in our lives. When we come to ask the Lord, 'Increase our faith', we are looking for freedom from pride and self-centredness.

Faith friends

1. *Prayer.* The single most important help to an increase in faith is prayer. The two-fold purpose of prayer is:
a) To know that the Lord is with us. We use prayer for many other purposes but this is what it is for. And in this we have to recognise that listening is more important than speaking. In prayer we listen to life, to our own experience, to other people, to God's word and through that listening grow in awareness of what is really important in life. In prayer we listen so keenly that we can know and experience the Lord walking with us, talking to us, carrying us, urging us on to more, loving us.
b) The second purpose of prayer is to equip us with all that is needed to follow him ever more fully. 'Increase our faith' is not so much a desire for stronger beliefs as a request for greater freedom to follow him, to be like him in his Body, the Church. We cannot do that within our own resources. We can only do it through the power of God. And that power is there for us through prayer.

2. *Humility.* This doesn't mean thinking badly of ourselves or putting ourselves down. True humility is about giving God his proper place as the acknowledged centre of true human life.

Humility is about letting ourselves know the wonderful beauty of nature, the dignity of every human person, the wonderful goodness of those who love us and whom we love. Humility is the ability to revel in the joy of being alive and being in love. As we ask the Lord to 'Increase our faith' we are asking him to make us into that kind of joyful, hopeful, dynamic people.

Some Features

The Gospel Readings for these Sundays are from Luke 14-17. It can be helpful to read these chapters at the beginning and catch the spirit of adventure with the Lord that is ahead.

TWENTY-SECOND SUNDAY OF THE YEAR

THEME
He gathers the humble.

PRAYER FOCUS
Fill our hearts with love of you
Question: What fills your heart right now?

READINGS

1) Ecclesiasticus 3:17-20; 28-29
Be gentle in carrying out your business
Question: In what ways do you need to grow in gentleness?

2) Response (to Psalm 67)
In your goodness, O God, you prepared a home for the poor.
Pray this response until you feel part of it.

3) Hebrews 12:18-19; 22-24
You have come to the city of the living God.
Question: Do you ever feel a sense of awe in the presence of
God? When? How does it feel?

4) Luke 14:1; 7-14
Repayment will be made to you when the virtuous rise again
Question: How does selfishness make it difficult for you to be
generous with others?

QUESTIONS FOR ACTION

For Married Couples: What are some of the best things about
your wife/husband in recent times? Tell her/him this week in
some special way.

For Others: How can you be of service to the poor this week?

TWENTY-THIRD SUNDAY OF THE YEAR

THEME
He gives, and asks for, everything.

PRAYER FOCUS
Give us true freedom
Question: In what ways are you not free?

READINGS

1) Wisdom 9:13-18
The reasonings of mortals are unsure:
and our intentions unstable.
Question: How do you react to this statement?

2) Response (to Psalm 89)
O Lord, you have been our refuge from one generation
to the next.
Pray this until you can feel the comfort of it.

3) Philemon 9-10; 12-17
Welcome him as you would me.
Question: How selective is your loving?

4) Luke 14:25-33
None of you can be my disciple unless you give up
all your possessions.
Question: What, in practice, is more important to you than the
Lord?

QUESTIONS FOR ACTION

For Married Couples: What will you sacrifice this week so as to
love your wife/husband in a special way?

For Others: What will you give away this week to someone in
need?

TWENTY–FOURTH SUNDAY OF THE YEAR

THEME
He welcomes sinners.

PRAYER FOCUS
May we serve you with all our heart and
know your forgiveness in our lives.
Question: In what ways do you feel the need for forgiveness?

READINGS

1) Exodus 32:7-11; 13-14
'I can see how headstrong these people are'.
Question: In what ways are people today headstrong in
not listening to God's ways?

2) Response (to Psalm 50)
I will leave this place and go to my father
Pray this until you feel the sense of it.

3) 1 Timothy 1:12-17
Christ Jesus came into the world to save sinners
Question: In what ways do you need salvation?

4) Luke 15:1-32
'This man welcomes sinners and eats with them.'
Question: Do you know anyone who is arrogant and
self-righteous? How do they affect you?

QUESTIONS FOR ACTION

For Married Couples: In what ways do you need forgiveness
from your wife/husband? How will you work on it this week?

For Others: Make a special effort for the sacrament of
confession/penance this week.

TWENTY-FIFTH SUNDAY OF THE YEAR

THEME
Lord of the oppressed.

PRAYER FOCUS
May we love one another and come to the perfection
prepared for us
Question: What limits do you set in your love for those closest to
you?

READINGS

1) Amos 8:4-7
'Never will I forget a single thing you have done.'
Question: In what ways do you see hypocrisy in the Church
and in society?

2) Response (to Psalm 112)
Praise the Lord, who raises the poor
Pray this response until you experience the freedom of it.

3) Timothy 2:1-8
He wants everyone to be saved and reach full knowledge
of the truth.
Question: What prevents you, and others, from facing full truth?

4) Luke 16:1-13
You cannot be the slave both of God and of money.
Question: What does this mean in your life?

QUESTIONS FOR ACTION

For Married Couples: What was one of the nicest things about
your courtship days? How could you relive that together this
week?

For Others: What could you do this week to register protest
against some injustice in the Church or in society?

TWENTY-SIXTH SUNDAY OF THE YEAR

THEME
A Witness for the truth.

PRAYER FOCUS
Continue to fill us with your gifts of love
Question: How eager are you for this prayer to be answered in
your own life and in your parish?

READINGS

1) Amos 6:1; 4-7
The sprawler's revelry is over!
Question: What makes people self-centred and selfish.

2) Response (to Psalm 145)
My soul, give praise to the Lord.
Pray this response until you feel the freedom of it.

3) 1 Timothy 6:11-16
Be filled with faith and love, patient and gentle.
Question: How do you need to change so as to be more patient
and gentle with people in your life?

4) Luke 16:19-31
They will not be convinced even if someone should rise from
the dead.
Question: Why is it so difficult for so many people to know and
accept the truth of Jesus? Is it difficult for you?

QUESTIONS FOR ACTION
For Married Couples: What are 3 of your wife/husband's best
qualities at present? Tell her/him this week.

For Others: Choose one person who is close to you. How will
you affirm the goodness of that person this week?

TWENTY-SEVENTH SUNDAY OF THE YEAR

THEME
The gift of faith.

PRAYER FOCUS
Forgive our failings, keep us in your peace
and lead us in the way of salvation.
Question: How could you be more at peace in your life?

READINGS

1) Habakkuk 1:2-3; 2:2-4
The upright person will live by faithfulness.
Question: What makes you downhearted about life?

2) Response (to Psalm 94)
O that today you would listen to his voice!
Harden not your hearts.
Pray this response until you feel the power of it.

3) 2 Timothy 1:6-8; 13-14
Fan into a flame the gift that God gave you.
Question: What is the most important thing for you about your
faith?

4) Luke 17:5-10
The Apostles said to the Lord: 'Increase our faith.'
Question: In what ways could your faith be increased and
strengthened?

QUESTIONS FOR ACTION
For Married Couples: What is one of the best gifts of life you
wife/husband has brought to you in marriage? How will you
acknowledge that this week?

For Others: How could you grow in some aspect of faith this
week?

SECTION 9

28th Sunday - Christ the King

Introduction

Say thanks

'What do you say?' is a favourite question of parents to their little children as they train them to say 'thank you' and so help them to be grateful for what they have. If only the adults would practice what they preach what a wonderful world we would have!

Why say thanks?

Listen to the radio any day during the week and you are put in touch with so much pain in people's lives all over the country. Nothing seems to be right. There is a lot of injustice in our society. There is a lot of pain in people's lives from broken relationships. There is a lot of betrayal from people who should be trustworthy. All these things need to be attended to. But there is also a lot more in life that can be lost sight of when our attention is taken over by what is wrong.

Reasons for thankfulness

1. *Life.* As we come towards the end of another year, it is important to look at so much we can and should be thankful for and put saying thanks into practice in preparation for the new year ahead. How many people waken up in the morning and say, 'Oh God, not again. Another day to be got through.' It's not that we want to be dead. It's that we don't want to be alive either! What a difference it would make if we practised saying thanks to God for the gift of life first thing every morning. We would learn to appreciate the adventure of life again and be able to look forward to each new day with all its possibilities.

2. *Nature.* The world we live in is an absolute wonder in its variety of sights and sounds and smells. So many of us are too busy to even notice it. Just take a few minutes today to do nothing but

look, listen, enjoy the place you are in. Even in the heart of the city there is so much that we can be thankful for in God's creation for us.

3. *People.* Most people live their lives in a family setting. When people are that close to you day after day they get on your nerves, they hurt you, they can alienate you. The result is so much criticism of one another in family life. Or you get so used to someone who lives close to you that you take her/him for granted. This is even worse than criticism. The fact is that each person we are close to has so much goodness and beauty that remains unacknowledged. What a difference it would make in family life if we practised saying thanks. Our homes would be aglow with joy.

4. *The Church.* The Church is full of sinners. That's what it is for. And yet we always seem shocked when someone is found out. The Church has given us one of the most precious gifts of life, the gift of faith. Through this gift we come to honour Christ living in us and among us. Because of this gift we become familiar with Mary and with the saints. Through the Church we have the Eucharist as a food of life and the forgiveness of our sins as the freedom to look ahead. There is so much wrong with the Church and there always will be. But there is so much beauty and goodness that we can and should be thankful for.

5. *Our parish.* In every parish community there are wonderful people who give their time and energy to the service of God and of those in need. From the way we talk you wouldn't think that is true! Many people don't talk about their community at all but just take all that's on offer and selfishly move on. Others talk only in criticism of what's wrong. The single most powerful force for renewing any parish is to develop a spirit of thankfulness in which everyone, the priests included, are acknowledged and confirmed in their goodness constantly.

Thank you for using this book for yourself or in your leadership of others. May you have all God's choicest blessings in the months and years ahead.

Some Features

The Gospel Readings for this series are from Luke 17-23. By reading these chapters and reflecting on them you will find so much more for which to be thankful.

TWENTY-EIGHTH SUNDAY OF THE YEAR

THEME
Thanksgiving.

PRAYER FOCUS
Make your love the foundation of our lives
Question: Do you want that prayer answered? How? Why?

READINGS

1) 2 Kings 5:14-17
'Now I know there is no God except in Israel.'
Question: What has been your best experience of God's love and power?

2) Response (to Psalm 97)
The Lord has shown his salvation to the nations.
Pray this response until you know the truth of it.

3) 2 Timothy 2:8-13
They cannot chain up God's news.
Question: What makes it difficult for the Gospels to be preached fully today?

4) Luke 17:11-19
'The other nine, where are they?'
Question: How much do you take God's gifts of live and love for granted? What can you do about it?

QUESTIONS FOR ACTION

For Married Couples: In what ways do you take your wife/ husband for granted? How will you change that this week?

For Others: Think of one or two people who have given you a lot in your life. How can you thank them this week?

TWENTY-NINTH SUNDAY OF THE YEAR

THEME
The power of prayer.

PRAYER FOCUS
Give us strength and joy in serving you
Question: Do you think of your daily life as serving God? What
does it mean to you?

READINGS

1) Exodus 17:8-13
As long as Moses kept his arms raised,
Israel had the advantage.
Question: Do you believe in the power of prayer for our world?
How do you exercise this power?

2) Response (to Psalm 120)
Our help is in the name of the Lord
who made heaven and earth.
Pray this until you are in touch with the power of God.

3) 2 Timothy 3:14-4:2
Proclaim the message and, welcome or unwelcome, insist on it.
Question: Why do people reject the gospel or water it down?

4) Luke 18:1-8
A parable about the need to pray continually and not lose heart.
Question: What things make you lose heart and tempt you to
give up?

QUESTIONS FOR ACTION

For Married Couples: In what way could you listen more fully to
your wife/husband this week?

For Others: How will you make special time for prayer each day
this week?

THIRTIETH SUNDAY OF THE YEAR

THEME
The Lord our judge.

PRAYER FOCUS
May we do with loving hearts what you ask of us
Question: What does 'a loving heart' mean to you?

READINGS

1) Ecclesiasticus 35:12-14; 16-19
The Lord is a judge who is no respecter of personages.
Question: Are you ever afraid of God? When? Why?

2) Response (to Psalm 33)
This poor man called; the Lord **heard** him.
Pray this until you experience the certainty of it.

3) 2 Timothy 4:6-8; 16-18
The Lord will rescue me from all evil attempts on me.
Question: Do you ever doubt the justice of God when things go
wrong? When has this happened?

4) Luke 18:9-14
'God, be merciful to me, a sinner.'
Question: What kind of judgement do you make on yourself?
How does it differ from how you judge others?

QUESTIONS FOR ACTION

For Married Couples: What have been some of the nicest things
about your wife/husband this month? How will you tell
her/him this week?

For Others: How will you bring help and comfort to someone in
need this week?

THIRTY-FIRST SUNDAY OF THE YEAR

THEME
The Lord of compassion.

PRAYER FOCUS
May we live the faith we profess.
Question: How do you need to make your faith more effective in
your daily life?

READINGS

1) Wisdom 11:22-12, 2
In your sight, Lord, the whole world is like a grain of dust that
tips the scales.
Question: To what extent do you appreciate the power of God
and the arrogance of people?

2) Response (to Psalm 144)
I will bless your name forever, O God my king.
Let this response open you up to the wonder of God.

3) Thessalonians 1:11-2, 2
Do not get excited too soon or alarmed by any prediction or
rumour implying that the day of the Lord has already arrived.
Question: How do you handle talk about the end of the world?

4) Luke 19:1-10
They all complained: 'He has gone to stay at a sinner's house.'
Question: How arrogant are you in your judgement of other
people?

QUESTIONS FOR ACTION

For Married Couples: In what ways could you surprise your
wife/husband in your love this week?

For Others: To whom could you show special kindness this
week?

THIRTY-SECOND SUNDAY OF THE YEAR

THEME
Our source of hope.

PRAYER FOCUS
Give us freedom of spirit
Question: What limits your freedom of spirit?

READINGS

1) Maccabees 7:1-2; 9-14
'We are prepared to die rather than break the law
of our ancestors.'
Question: What do you think of faith like that?

2) Response (to Psalm 16)
I shall be filled when I awake, with the sight
of your glory, O Lord.
Pray this until you catch the spirit of hope in it.

3) 2 Thessalonians 2:16-3:5
The Lord is faithful and he will strengthen you and guard you
from the evil one.
Question: How do you need to be guarded from the evil one?

4) Luke 20:27-38
He is God, not of the dead, but of the living.

QUESTIONS FOR ACTION
For Married Couples: How could you make your sexual
relationship more life-giving for your wife/husband this week?
For Others: To whom could you bring hope and joy this week?

THIRTY-THIRD SUNDAY OF THE YEAR

THEME
The triumph of God.

PRAYER FOCUS
Keep us faithful in serving you.
Question: What does this prayer mean to you?

READINGS

1) Micah 3:19-20
All the arrogant and evil doers will be like stubble.
Question: Do you believe that the good will triumph?
Do you ever doubt it? When?

2) Response (to Psalm 97)
The Lord comes to rule the people with fairness
Pray this so as to experience the freedom it brings.

3) 2 Thessalonians 3:7-12
Do not let anyone have food if he refuses to work.
Question: Do you ever feel taken for granted? When?

4) Luke 21:5-19
When you hear of wars and revolutions do not be frightened.
Question: When have you experienced the presence of
God with you? What was it like?

QUESTIONS FOR ACTION

For Married Couples: What would you have most liked to have
said to your wife/husband at the end of your life? Say it this
week.

For Others: Is there anyone with whom you need to reconcile?
How can you do it this week?

LAST SUNDAY OF THE YEAR

THEME
Christ the King.

PRAYER FOCUS
May all in heaven and earth acclaim your glory.
Question: Do you want the whole world filled with God's glory?

READINGS

1) 2 Samuel 5:1-3
You are the man who shall be shepherd of my people.
Question: How conscious are you of the presence of Christ in
your daily life? How can you grow in this?

2) Response (to Psalm 121)
I rejoiced when I heard them say – 'Let us go to God's house.'
Pray this until the joy of it is in your own heart.

3) Colossians 1:11-20
The Church is his body, he is its head.
Question: How conscious are you of your privilege in belonging
to the Church? How can you grow in this?

4) Luke 23:35-43
'Jesus, remember me when you come into your kingdom.'
Question: How conscious are you of your need for forgiveness
and healing? How can you grow in this?

QUESTIONS FOR ACTION

For Married Couples: In what ways do you need to give to and to
ask for forgiveness from your wife/husband?

For Others: How could you do something to help the environment this week?